WILLIAM GAMINARA

William Gaminara is an actor and playwright. His other plays
include *According to Hoyle*, *Back Up the Hearse and Let Them
Smell the Flowers* (Hampstead Theatre) and an adaptation of
Zola's *Germinal* (Paines Plough). His work for film and
television includes *This Life*, *The Lakes* and *Ella and the
Mothers*.

T0346669

## Other Titles in this Series

William Gaminara

# THE THREE LIONS

NICK HERN BOOKS

London

www.nickhernbooks.co.uk

**A Nick Hern Book**

*The Three Lions* first published in Great Britain in 2013 as a paperback original by Nick Hern Books Limited, The Glasshouse, 49a Goldhawk Road, London W12 8QP

*The Three Lions* copyright © 2013 William Gaminara

William Gaminara has asserted his right to be identified as the author of this work

Cover image: Sam Smith
Cover design: Ned Hoste, 2H

Typeset by Nick Hern Books, London
Printed and bound in Great Britain by Mimeo Ltd, Huntingdon, Cambridgeshire PE29 6XX

A CIP catalogue record for this book is available from the British Library

ISBN 978 1 84842 351 0

*The Three Lions* was first performed on 31 July 2013 at the Pleasance Beyond as part of the Edinburgh Festival Fringe. The cast, in alphabetical order, was as follows:

| | |
|---|---|
| VIKRAM/ASHOK | Ravi Aujla |
| PENNY | Alice Bailey-Johnson |
| DAVID BECKHAM | Sean Browne |
| DAVID CAMERON | Dugald Bruce-Lockhart |
| LACHLAN | Lewis Collier |
| PRINCE WILLIAM | Tom Davey |

| | |
|---|---|
| *Director* | Philip Wilson |
| *Designer* | Colin Falconer |
| *Lighting Designer* | Malcolm Rippeth |
| *Video Designer* | Ben Harvey |
| *Production Manager* | Simon Robertson |
| *Sound Designer* | Jessica Kelley |
| *DSM* | Rachel Gillard |
| *Costume Assistant* | Rosy Emmerich |
| *Producers* | Jenny Topper |
| | Rosie Bowen for PBJ Management |

With thanks to Edward Bennett, Oliver Birch, Anthony Clark, Rupert Farley, Raj Ghatak, Alexander Hanson and also to Richard Johnson, Terry Johnson

**Characters**

PENNY
VIKRAM
DAVID CAMERON
DAVID BECKHAM
PRINCE WILLIAM
ASHOK
LACHLAN

VIKRAM *and* ASHOK *should be played by the same actor.*

*This text went to press before the end of rehearsals and so may differ slightly from the play as performed.*

**Scene One**

*The night before the announcement of the host nation for the 2018 FIFA World Cup. The lights go up on a smart, medium-sized en suite room in a Zurich hotel. The room contains three chairs, a small table, a sofa and a desk, on top of which there is a bowl of fruit and a football. A side door leads off to the bedroom. The main door opens and a young woman, PENNY, is shown in by VIKRAM, an Indian porter, pulling a modest wheelie-bag. DAVID CAMERON follows, talking on his mobile phone.*

VIKRAM. Here we are.

CAMERON (*on phone*). They missed the flight...!

VIKRAM. Heating, air conditioning...

PENNY. Very good.

CAMERON (*on phone*). All flights are cancelled...

PENNY. Cancelled!

CAMERON (*on phone*). Great.

VIKRAM. Television, DVD player... minibar.

  VIKRAM *goes into the bedroom.*

CAMERON (*on phone*). Well, Penny is here and I'm sure will be more than capable of stepping up to the plate. She's got me as far as the hotel so she must be doing something right...

VIKRAM (*off*). Bathroom, shower.

PENNY (*going into the bedroom*). Right.

CAMERON (*on phone*)....okay, keep me in touch. I said... hello... hello? (*Off phone.*) Even better.

PENNY (*reappearing*). They're not coming?

CAMERON. Not just yet anyway. Don't worry, you'll be fine.

*He passes her to take a look in the bedroom.*

(*Off.*) Oh.

PENNY. Yes I know, did you actually ask for...

CAMERON (*coming out*). No I didn't. I think there must be some kind of mistake. It should be a double.

VIKRAM. Twin, no?

*He gets out a piece of paper and shows it to* CAMERON *and* PENNY.

You see? Twin. For sharing.

*He points to the document.*

CAMERON. No, no sharing. I definitely asked for a double. (*To* VIKRAM.) One person, yes? And one big bed. (*To* PENNY.) Either way, we need to change as...

VIKRAM. This is you, yes?

CAMERON. Yes.

VIKRAM. Sharing.

CAMERON. No. I'm not... Ah, I think I see what's happened. I'm not William Hague. I don't think he's coming.

VIKRAM. Oh. And Mr... Clegg?

CAMERON. He's definitely not coming.

VIKRAM. The Prime Minister is not coming?

PENNY. Yes.

CAMERON. The Prime Minister is here. I...

PENNY. This is the Prime Minister.

VIKRAM. You *are* Mr Hague?

CAMERON. No.

VIKRAM. You are Mr Cl...

CAMERON. Clegg, no. I am Mr Cameron.

VIKRAM. Forgive me, sir, I have no interest in politics whatsoever.

CAMERON. Evidently.

VIKRAM. What you don't know, you can't speak of.

CAMERON. No. Penny, perhaps you could sort this out please, ASAP.

PENNY. Yes, I'm so sorry. (*Taking* VIKRAM *aside*.) We need to change to a double room for the Prime Minister Mr Cameron.

CAMERON. That's me.

PENNY. As soon as possible. A double bed in a double room.

VIKRAM. You will have to speak to reception.

PENNY. Right. Well, I will go and do that now.

*She hesitates.*

CAMERON. What is it?

PENNY. Swiss isn't exactly my first language.

CAMERON. It isn't anyone's first language. Not even the Swiss. I'll wait here.

PENNY *leaves.* CAMERON *is left with* VIKRAM, *who doesn't leave.*

VIKRAM. Air conditioning, television, DVD player…

CAMERON. Yes, you've done that already.

VIKRAM. Minibar.

CAMERON. Right.

VIKRAM. Anything else, sir?

CAMERON. Apart from the correct room, no.

VIKRAM *straightens the bag.*

VIKRAM. Small bag, but very heavy.

CAMERON. Oh. Right. It's not that heavy actually, but...

*He puts his hand in his pocket. No change. He has only got a note.*

Unfortunately I've only...

*He hesitates, then has an idea. Digs in his pocket and produces a pound coin. He hands it to him.*

There we go.

VIKRAM *stares at it.*

VIKRAM. Sterling?

CAMERON. I think you'll find it works. Unlike a lot of other currencies round here.

*VIKRAM exits, unimpressed. CAMERON has a quick look round the room and out of the window. He picks up the ball, throws it around a couple of times and then places it idly at his feet. He does a couple of kick-ups before it falls. He tries a trick and almost falls over... in the middle of which, DAVID BECKHAM walks in.*

David, hello! Caught me red-handed, red-footed rather, just seeing if I could still do some of the old tricks. Great to see you again, how are you?

BECKHAM. I'm good thanks, yeah.

CAMERON. You're looking good. Very fit.

BECKHAM. Yeah, well... I do my best. Doesn't get any easier.

CAMERON. Tell me about it. So you flew over in your own...

BECKHAM. Yeah. Easier really.

CAMERON. Yes. (*Beat.*) How's the family?

BECKHAM. They're good, very good.

CAMERON. Excellent. You've got the three now, haven't you? Brooklyn, Cruz and... Elvis?

BECKHAM. Romeo.

CAMERON. Romeo, sorry.

BECKHAM. Yeah. After the character by Shakespeare?

CAMERON. Right.

BECKHAM. Number Four on the way.

CAMERON. Really? Congratulations. Keep going and you'll have your own team.

BECKHAM. Yeah. What about yours?

CAMERON. Fine. Arthur, Florence and Eleanor. All thriving. We should get them together some time. They could all... (*Beat*.) you know...

BECKHAM. Yeah.

*Pause*.

CAMERON. So, all set for tomorrow?

BECKHAM. Yeah, I hope so. Bit of, you know, work to do.

CAMERON. Just a bit, yes, but hey, that's why we're here.

BECKHAM. Am I in the right room only...

CAMERON. Oh sorry. This is *your* room, is it? I'm so sorry, I didn't realise... no, there's been a bit of a mix-up. I've been parked here temporarily while they try and sort it out but I'll get out of your way...

VIKRAM *arrives, pulling a trolley with three large bags, all belonging to* BECKHAM.

BECKHAM (*to* VIKRAM). Just here'll do. Cheers.

CAMERON. Yes, they seem to have got us down as sharing a room somehow.

BECKHAM. Tabloids will love that.

CAMERON. Wouldn't they just. You're alright with a twin then, are you?

BECKHAM. Not fussed really. So long as there's a bed and a bath.

VIKRAM. Air conditioning, TV, DVD player, minibar, bathroom. (*Beat*.) Mirror.

*He waits to be tipped.* BECKHAM *finds a pound coin in his pocket.*

BECKHAM. I've only…

*He roots around again.*

Ah no. It's alright. There you go.

*He takes out a note and gives it to the* PORTER.

VIKRAM. Thank you, sir. Thank you so much. Would you be so kind as to sign your autograph?

BECKHAM. Yeah, sure.

VIKRAM *hands him a notebook.*

Just here?

VIKRAM. Please. To 'Vikram Hiremath'.

BECKHAM. Vikram. Good name.

VIKRAM. Thank you, sir. It means 'the soul of discretion'.

BECKHAM. Yeah? Very nice. (*Writing*.) 'To Vikram…'

VIKRAM. And 'Hiremath'. That means 'the Lord of Om'.

BECKHAM. The Lord of…?

VIKRAM. Om.

BECKHAM. Om. What… where's that then?

VIKRAM. Oh, it's not a place. It's a sound.

BECKHAM. Right. So 'To Vikram Hiremath…'

VIKRAM. 'With best wishes…'

BECKHAM. 'With best wishes…'

VIKRAM. 'Wayne Rooney.'

BECKHAM. Wayne… wait a second… I'm not…

CAMERON. Don't worry, I had exactly the same thing.

BECKHAM. He thought you was Wayne Rooney?

CAMERON. No but…

VIKRAM. You are not Mr Rooney?

BECKHAM. No.

VIKRAM. You are?

BECKHAM. I'm David Beckham.

VIKRAM. David…?

BECKHAM. Beckham.

VIKRAM. Forgive me, sir, I know nothing about football.

BECKHAM. Right. Do you still want me to…?

VIKRAM. But of course, sir, of course.

　　BECKHAM *signs and hands it back.* VIKRAM *reads it.*

　　'David Beckham.' And what does Beckham mean?

BECKHAM. Oh, nothing. As far as I know.

VIKRAM. 'Nothing.'

BECKHAM. No, it doesn't actually mean 'nothing'… it's… it's…

VIKRAM. It's meaningless.

BECKHAM. Yeah.

VIKRAM. I see. So, Mr Cameron…

CAMERON (*assuming the same request for an autograph*). Oh, go on then.

VIKRAM (*putting the notebook away*). Reception are dealing with your request.

CAMERON. Oh right. Glad to hear it.

　　VIKRAM *leaves.*

　　Bloody hell.

BECKHAM. Not big on football in India, are they.

CAMERON. Or politicians apparently. It's really not good enough.

BECKHAM. You still play a bit though, do you?

CAMERON. If only. Don't have the time, I'm afraid. I've also got two left feet which doesn't help.

BECKHAM. Two left feet?

CAMERON. Not literally, no! No, that would be… Anyhow, here we all are or will be shortly. Listen, I don't have to tell you that…

PENNY *enters*.

PENNY. Prime Minister… I've had a word about the room but I'm afraid there's going to be a bit of a delay. I've spoken to… (*Sees* BECKHAM.) Oh, hello.

BECKHAM. Hello.

PENNY. It's… golly… it's you. Sorry, am I…?

BECKHAM. No.

PENNY. Yes. Gosh. Yes, Prime Minister, there's…

CAMERON. Penny, just call me David. We're all, you know… (*To* BECKHAM.) Penny's a recent addition to the team, most of whom have managed to get themselves stranded on the runway at Gatwick.

BECKHAM. Oh dear.

PENNY. Yes. (*Beat*.) Anyway, there's been a bit of a… a monumental cock-up, 'scuse my French. They're actually fully booked, though there is like an annexe apparently, for overspill, but yes, they're shifting things around so it should only take another fifteen days or so.

CAMERON. Fifteen days!

PENNY. Yes. Sorry, *minutes*. Minutes obviously, sorry. But you can always use my corridor in the meantime if need be… room, I mean. My room's just along the corridor, down at the end on the left.

CAMERON. Right.

PENNY. 427.

CAMERON. Excellent.

PENNY. That's the number.

CAMERON. We haven't got a huge amount of time, so…

BECKHAM. Why don't you wait here till your room's sorted then, you know… we can get going while you're waiting.

CAMERON. If you're sure you're alright with that? That would be great.

BECKHAM. Yeah that's fine. Obviously I'm not going anywhere.

PENNY. Oh good.

CAMERON. Okay. Now food and drink. Can you get hold of someone?

PENNY. Yes.

CAMERON. And can it *not* be Vikram, please.

PENNY. Oh. I rather think he's been, like, assigned to us.

CAMERON. Then please inform him he's been unassigned. We're underwhelmed to put it mildly, aren't we? If we could have someone who knows who and what we are…

BECKHAM. Well…

CAMERON. And do we know if Prince William has arrived yet?

PENNY. Prince who?

CAMERON. William.

PENNY. Prince William, yes of course, I mean, I don't know but I'll see if I can find out.

CAMERON. He'll be in the Presidential Suite. If he has, can you send him along.

PENNY. Right.

CAMERON. And discreetly. I do not want the press sniffing round us in any shape or form. That is your responsibility.

PENNY. I'll get straight onto it. (*To* BECKHAM.) I know it's rather cheeky but would you mind awfully if I got an autograph.

CAMERON. Penny...

PENNY. I know, it must be *so* boring for you...

BECKHAM. That's alright.

PENNY. And I always feel so sorry for people who have to, like... especially tennis players, I mean, there they are, they've just played five sets or whatever and then they're expected to sign their names about four hundred times, I'm surprised their hands don't drop off. There again, you play with your feet so... I don't suppose that's a problem, unless you sign autographs with your feet. Or play football with your hands like Madonna.

BECKHAM. Maradona.

CAMERON. Penny.

PENNY. Maradona! I'm sorry, I'm talking absolute rubbish, aren't I.

BECKHAM. No worries. Anywhere special?

PENNY. How do you mean?

BECKHAM. There was this girl last week who wanted me to autograph her bum.

PENNY. No! Really!

BECKHAM. Yeah.

PENNY. How weird is that!

BECKHAM. Brought her own felt-tips and everything.

CAMERON. And did you?

BECKHAM. No. I was with Brooklyn, so...

PENNY. Oh no, not really appropriate.

BECKHAM. No.

PENNY. Still, nice to be asked. I imagine. No, tempted as I am, a piece of your bum will be fine. *Paper*, sorry.

*He grabs a piece of hotel stationery and signs it.*

Thank you so much. Golly. Lovely to meet you. I'll chase up Prince Harry.

CAMERON. William.

PENNY. William. Sorry. It was a very early start.

*She smiles and leaves.*

CAMERON. Trainee. In case you hadn't guessed.

BECKHAM. Do you mind if I unpack some of this stuff? Only you want it on hangers as soon as you can else it creases up.

CAMERON. Please do. Blimey. Sure you've brought enough clothes?

BECKHAM. Should be alright. We're only here one night, aren't we?

BECKHAM *takes something carefully out of the first suitcase and puts it to one side.*

CAMERON. What are those?

BECKHAM. Crystals.

CAMERON. Oh right.

BECKHAM. Yeah. Pink quartz and black tourmaline? Very lucky.

CAMERON. Well. I'm not going to argue with that. I suspect we're going to need all the luck we can get.

BECKHAM*'s mobile phone rings.*

BECKHAM (*on phone*). Hello, babe. (*Beat.*) Yeah, about a half-hour ago… (*Beat.*) No, I'm hanging them up now… (*Beat.*) It's alright… (*Beat.*) Single bed, yeah, it's a twin, actually… (*Beat.*) I didn't ask for it… (*Beat.*) No one!… No one, I'm telling you. Well, there *is* someone as it happens right now but… (*Beat.*) No… no it's not actually… listen then:

*He holds up the phone towards* CAMERON.

Say something, will you.

CAMERON. What?

BECKHAM. Doesn't matter what, just speak.

CAMERON. Hello. David Cameron here.

BECKHAM *puts the phone back to his ear.*

BECKHAM (*on phone*). See? Male. (*Beat.*) David Cameron. (*Beat.*) The Prime Minister? (*Beat.*) England. Listen, babe, I've got to go. (*Beat.*) No, not yet. I haven't even seen him yet… (*Beat.*) Well, I can't just like, *ask* him, can I… (*Beat.*) I will yeah… promise… alright, love ya. Bye. (*To* CAMERON.) Bloody hell. She's desperate to get an invite to the Royal Wedding. Don't give a damn about the World Cup.

*He starts taking clothes out of the suitcase and carrying them through into the bedroom.* CAMERON *wanders over to the window.*

CAMERON. Of course, they're all in the Baur au Lac Hotel. The FIFA crowd. £2,400 a suite. Who would have thought one little duck-house and a moat could do so much damage.

BECKHAM (*off*). This is alright. I've been in worse.

*He comes back in, holding a suit.*

Now I thought this would do for the first meeting tonight, yeah?

CAMERON. Oh right. Yes. A suit seems… suitable.

BECKHAM. And then the second meeting, I thought maybe same kind of thing but in blue and a much narrower lapel…

if I can find it. Obviously a bit more Euro, bit more, you know…

*A text comes through on* BECKHAM*'s phone.*

Woah… Guess what.

CAMERON. What?

BECKHAM (*reading*). Ronaldo has had to pull out of the Spanish–Portuguese bid. Twisted his ankle.

CAMERON. Oh, that is bad luck.

BECKHAM. Yeah.

*They catch each other's eye and start to laugh/celebrate.*

CAMERON. Now now. Enough of that.

BECKHAM (*more text has come through*). Ladbrokes have lengthened their odds from five to two to eleven to four.

CAMERON. Have they now!

*A knock on the door.* BECKHAM *opens it to* PRINCE WILLIAM.

WILLIAM. Hello!

BECKHAM. Hi.

BECKHAM *offers a high-five.* WILLIAM *responds slightly awkwardly but loving it.*

How's it all going?

WILLIAM. Oh, you know, pretty damn good.

CAMERON. William, hello, great to see you. You two know each other presumably.

BECKHAM. We've met two or three times, haven't we. Wembley, Wembley and…

WILLIAM. Wembley I think.

BECKHAM. Yeah, probably. Still supporting Aston Villa?

CAMERON. Nothing wrong with Aston Villa.

WILLIAM. Still playing for LA Galaxy?

*They laugh.*

Apparently Ronaldo's pulled out of the Spanish–Portuguese bid with a twisted ankle.

CAMERON. Yes, so we heard.

WILLIAM. Rotten bad luck. (*Beat.*) For him.

*Again they laugh/celebrate.*

CAMERON. Good to know we're all singing from the same hymn sheet. And talking of hymn sheets, congratulations again on the engagement, excellent news.

WILLIAM. Thanks very much, bit scary but… you know.

BECKHAM. Just get a couple of drinks inside you beforehand, you'll be fine.

CAMERON. Settled on a date yet?

WILLIAM. No, not yet.

BECKHAM. Lots of decisions.

WILLIAM. Yah.

BECKHAM. When… Where.

WILLIAM. Yah.

BECKHAM. Who.

WILLIAM. Er no, it's definitely going to be Kate.

BECKHAM. To invite, I mean.

WILLIAM. Yeah, no, I know I was…

BECKHAM. Big do?

WILLIAM. Not massive. There's a bit of recession on at the moment? So Gran's really putting her foot down.

BECKHAM. What are you going to wear?

WILLIAM. Haven't really thought about it to be honest. Birthday suit probably.

BECKHAM. Yeah? What colour?

WILLIAM (*to* CAMERON). Actually I meant to have a chat with you about Bank Holidays.

BECKHAM. Go for a Saturday. Every time. Sleep it off Sunday.

WILLIAM. Yah.

BECKHAM. A weekday is cheaper though. Swings and roundabouts.

CAMERON. All in good time. Now I'm actually roomless at the moment, William, but I thought it would be a good idea as we haven't got that much time if we cracked on with things, if that's alright with you.

WILLIAM. Absolutely.

CAMERON. David, do you want to pull up a chair?

BECKHAM. Sure.

CAMERON. How was the journey, by the way?

WILLIAM. Very good, very smooth.

CAMERON. Did you come in your own…

WILLIAM. Yes.

CAMERON. Great. Room okay?

WILLIAM. Fine. Bit poky. But fine.

CAMERON. Good. Good. Least you've got one.

WILLIAM. Oh?

CAMERON. Don't ask.

*He doesn't. They are now all three sat on chairs in the middle of the room.* CAMERON*'s is slightly lower than the others.*

Right. We're off. Well, welcome to both of you, first off I can't tell you how thrilled I am to be part of this particular 'dream' team, if I may call it that… whatever the outcome, the sheer pedigree that we three can bring to the table is... as our friends across the water would say... 'awesome', *but*... and it's a big 'but'... I would be lying if I told you that this was even *close* to being a done deal. What I *can* say, is that when asked by Tessa Jowell to support a London 2012 Olympic bid, Tony Blair said... and I quote: 'Yes, but suppose we get beaten and, what's worse, we get beaten by the French and end up being humiliated?' Now, those, if I may say so, were the words of a loser and just in case I haven't made it clear, I am not here to lose, I am here to win. And the key to winning as ever lies in the preparation. We do not want to be caught so to speak with our trousers down.

*There is a knock at the door.*

Ah. With a bit of luck that's my accommodation sorted.

*He opens it. An Indian man stands there. He is the spitting image of* VIKRAM, *though dressed more traditionally. He speaks with a strong Indian accent.*

ASHOK. Mr David Cameron, sir, my name is Ashok Hiremath and I have been specially assigned to the British Delegation by the hotel management to cater for all your requirements, and to ensure that everything is completely tickety-boo.

CAMERON. Er...

ASHOK. I should say also, sir, that I am personally a very, very big fan of yours. You are the most important man in England today and by extension therefore in Europe if not the whole world. I have read all of your speeches wall to wall including those of the British pre-electoral debates where you so magnificently exposed the frailties of Gordon Brown and his faulty economic agenda. You most definitely have the gift of the gob.

CAMERON. That's very kind of you to say so but were you not here just a few minutes ago?

ASHOK. No no, sir, don't worry, you are not losing any of your marbles, that was my brother Vikram, sir, we are identical twins.

CAMERON. Ah, that would explain it.

ASHOK. Born not only on the same day but in the same place.

BECKHAM. You look exactly the same!

ASHOK. We do, sir, we do. Identical in fact. Two peas in a pod.
But I must apologise for my brother, between you, me and
the gatepost he has been at this hotel for far too long. He will
not trouble you again I give you my word. I myself came
over to join him from Delhi only one month ago. Sometimes
a fresh pair of legs is what is required. Is that not true, Mr
Beckham?

BECKHAM. Yeah.

ASHOK. It is a pleasure indeed to meet you, sir, such an
inspirational sports and fashion icon, the man who the
August edition of *Heat* magazine in 2007 voted the second
most sexy man in the world. Pipped at the post by Gary
Barlow. I have watched all your matches, every single one,
sir. My personal favourite if you don't mind my saying so,
sir, was the goal scored against Greece for the qualifying
round of the World Cup on October 6th 2001 in the dying
seconds of the game no less… in which you succeeded in
creating a trajectory for the ball that seemed to defy all
known mathematical principles. On that day you did truly
bend it… not like Beckham, but *as* Beckham, because that is
who you are. It is a privilege to meet you, sir.

BECKHAM. Thanks very much.

ASHOK. And last but by no means least, Your Royal Highness.
I follow all your engagements all over the world and, if you
will forgive my weak attempt at a pun, sir, none is more
pleasing than the recent marital engagement which you have
just announced to someone who, I believe in a break with
tradition, is a complete and utter slapper.

CAMERON. Commoner, commoner…

ASHOK. Commoner, I beg your pardon, sir, commoner…

*He shakes* WILLIAM*'s hand and holds on to it.*

I am honoured to shake your hand, sir, the same hand which will one day rule over Great Britain I am sure with fairness, determination and generosity... qualities inherited from the great kings and queens of England throughout the ages. To shake this hand, is to shake hands with history. Welcome to you all!

ALL. Thank you.

ASHOK. Now, I understand you would like some refreshments to help you with the great task ahead of you.

BECKHAM. You haven't got any crisps, have you...

ASHOK. Certainly, sir, any particular flavour.

BECKHAM. Cheese and onion.

ASHOK. My favourite, sir, any particular cheese?

BECKHAM. Er no.

ASHOK. Very good. Mr David Cameron, sir?

CAMERON. If there's a Pringle to be found that would be very welcome. Any flavour.

ASHOK. Pringles for you, sir. My favourite. Your Royal Highness?

WILLIAM. I think I'll have some pork scratchings if that's okay...

ASHOK. Pork scratchings. Very good, sir. Very *Tom Brown's School Days*. You're sure I can't tempt you with some smoked salmon canapés, caviar. Or devils on horseback if you would prefer? Or maybe even, for the sweeter tooth, a Kipling's Orange Cupcake?

CAMERON. You're joking.

ASHOK. What man could not say that if he were to die with a Kipling's Orange Cupcake in his hand, licking the remnants of the icing from the tinfoil, that he would not die a happy man?

WILLIAM. No, I'll go with the pork scratchings. If you have any.

ASHOK. Most certainly. And to drink… ginger beer? A nice cup of tea perhaps? 'If you are cold, tea will warm you. If you are too heated, it will cool you. If you are depressed, it will cheer you. If you are excited, it will calm you.' William Gladstone, 1865.

CAMERON. Go on then, tea all round, yes?

ASHOK. Very good. I will be back in a jiffy.

*He leaves.*

CAMERON. Well! I know which brother I prefer.

WILLIAM. Amazing!

BECKHAM. We should get him to do the bid tomorrow.

WILLIAM. Defo.

CAMERON. Anyhow, as I was saying before I was so… politely interrupted… thrilled as I am to have you guys on board, we have to be realistic. Spain and Portugal and Russia have their nose in front…

BECKHAM. Can I say something there?

CAMERON. Sure.

BECKHAM. I think you're right, we are behind, but at the end of the day, it is like Ashok was saying, in that match against Greece obviously we was two–one down with only minutes to play before that free kick but because people hung in there and didn't, you know, give up, bish bash bosh next thing you know we was qualified. I know it's been said before but at the end of the day it really isn't over until the final whistle.

CAMERON. Sure, well, I'm glad…

BECKHAM. Then again, we went on to meet Brazil in the quarters and obviously they was a good team and they went ahead after two minutes with Rivaldo, but again we didn't roll over, Michael Owen gets us right back in the game with a lovely little goal from out of nothing.

WILLIAM. So you won?

BECKHAM. No, in the end they scored two more, beat us three–one and knocked us out.

CAMERON. Yes. Leaving that particular game to one side for a moment, the second thing I want to say is with respect to the *Panorama* fiasco. Frankly, accusing FIFA publicly of being a bunch of crooks three days before our FIFA World Cup bid and the clue may I say is in the word 'FIFA'… is something of an own goal.

BECKHAM. I'd go further than that, David, without wanting to upset anyone, I'd say the BBC have completely fucked us. Wouldn't you?

WILLIAM. Yah, I haven't really… Yah, I suppose so.

BECKHAM. You don't mind my swearing like that, do you?

WILLIAM. Me? God no, I swear all the time. Effing this, effing that.

BECKHAM. They fucked us right up the arse.

CAMERON. Sure, sure, but what I want to say about that is that we can only have one focus here and that is trying to bring the World Cup to England.

WILLIAM. And they are only allegations anyway.

BECKHAM. The Spanish said this thing about, like when you point at someone, yeah, you always have three fingers pointing at yourself.

*He holds up his hand and points to show what he means.*

See, this one's pointing, yeah. At… whoever. But these three are pointing back towards me. See? So what I'm saying is the BBC can point away but in the end they're not just fucking us in the arse, they're fucking themselves in the arse as well.

CAMERON. Yes. I don't want to get too bogged down in who's doing what to whose… arse, the point I really want to make is that we're all members of the footballing family, and we should therefore express solidarity with Mr Blatter and his colleagues. It isn't going to do us any favours either having a pop at FIFA or for that matter the BBC. The fact is we have a robust, free press unlike some other countries I can think of and believe me I wouldn't have it any other way.

*The room phone rings.* BECKHAM *answers.*

BECKHAM (*on phone*). Hello. Yeah, he is, hold on. It's for you.

CAMERON. Who is it?

BECKHAM (*on phone*). Who is it, please? (*To* CAMERON.) It's Nick.

CAMERON. Nick who?

BECKHAM (*on phone*). Nick who? (*To* CAMERON.) Clegg.

CAMERON. Oh right.

*He hesitates but decides to take it.*

(*On phone.*) Hi, Nick. Yes, sorry about that, signal's a bit iffy. Everything okay your end… (*Beat.*) good. (*Beat.*) No really, I think just one of us out here is fine. (*Beat.*) David? Yes, that was him. I'm in his room as it happens. (*Beat.*) And Prince William, yes. (*Beat.*) I will say hello from you, yes. (*Beat.*) To both of them, yes. Listen, is there anything particular that you…

BECKHAM. Are you always called William?

CAMERON (*going into the bedroom*). We still don't know.

WILLIAM. How do you mean?

BECKHAM. I mean do you ever get called… Will, say?

CAMERON (*off*). I see.

WILLIAM. Not really. I was called Steve when I was at uni.

BECKHAM. Really?

WILLIAM. Steve Windsor, yah. For security. You know, if anything unexpected happened. Or like a bit of camouflage if I went out and got paralytic, you know.

CAMERON (*off*). Yes well, think of it more as an immigration cap rather than a quota.

BECKHAM. What about Bill?

WILLIAM. No.

BECKHAM. Willy?

WILLIAM. No.

BECKHAM. Wazza?

WILLIAM. No.

*They laugh.*

CAMERON (*off*). Perhaps that can wait till I get back.

BECKHAM. My mate Ian right, he calls everyone Wazza or Bazza or whatever. He just takes the first letter of their name and adds 'azza'. So if you was called, say Brian... you'd be Brazza.

WILLIAM. Oh so the first *two* letters.

BECKHAM. Yeah, so I'm Dazza, Gary... Neville... is Gazza... and you'd be... Wazza. Should've gone for that instead of Steve.

WILLIAM. Yah. No. Never been called that.

CAMERON (*off*). I'll be back in time for Prime Minister's questions... (*Beat.*) Quite sure... No really, no need, I'll definitely be back in time.

WILLIAM. Any more tattoos since I last saw you? You were about to...

BECKHAM. Oh yeah, a couple at least. I'm up to twelve now. Last time I looked anyways.

WILLIAM. Really, wow.

BECKHAM. Yeah, last one I had done was Jesus being carried by three cherubs?

WILLIAM. Yah?

BECKHAM. Yeah. Just next to my armpit. Obviously I've got three boys of my own, so the cherubs like represent *my* three boys?

WILLIAM. Right. Carrying?

BECKHAM. Me.

WILLIAM. Oh right.

BECKHAM. You know. When I get old or whatever.

CAMERON (*off*). If that's all...

BECKHAM. You ever thought of having one?

WILLIAM. No, not as such, no.

BECKHAM. I don't mean like 'Love' and 'Hate' on your knuckles or whatever but...

WILLIAM. No...

BECKHAM. More something like the name of your loved one across your chest?

WILLIAM. Not sure if I'd really like it.

BECKHAM (*spelling it out*). 'K–A–T–E' in great big letters across the front.

WILLIAM. 'Rex' maybe. One day.

BECKHAM. Rex. (*Beat.*) Not... not Kate?

WILLIAM. And then when... if... I ever get to be coronated, like you guys could run to the camera at the edge of the abbey and rip off my shirt... 'REX'!

BECKHAM. Right.

CAMERON (*coming back in, on phone*)....Well, that's because you're *not* Prime Minister, look, I have to go. Alright. Bye. (*To* BECKHAM *and* WILLIAM.) Sorry about that. Affairs of state. Let's crack on.

*A knock on the door.* PENNY *enters.*

PENNY. Hello again. (*Sees* WILLIAM.) Oh my God, hello. (*Half-curtsies.*)

WILLIAM. Hi. Who are you?

PENNY. Oh golly, I'm no one. I'm not, you know, a footballer or whatever.

CAMERON. Penny is part of our admin team, now, what news on my room?

PENNY. Oh right. Right, yes, there's good news and bad news. The good news is you have a room. The bad news is at the moment there's someone in it.

CAMERON. What do you mean?

PENNY. But it is a double room, double bed, double... everything.

CAMERON. Double-booked by the sound of it. Who is in it?

PENNY. A Portugueser.

CAMERON. A what?

PENNY. A man from Portugal.

CAMERON. Which bit of that is good? That sounds more to me like bad news and worse news. Why is there a man from Portugal in my room? Haven't they got their own rooms?

PENNY. Oh no, no, he's mending the shower.

CAMERON. Ah. So he's not an important man from Portugal if that's not a contradiction in terms.

PENNY. He will be gone by like... eight o'clock?

CAMERON. You're quite sure of that.

BECKHAM. If the worst comes to the worst you can kip in my room and I'll...

PENNY. Oh, that's so kind of you...

CAMERON. David, I would not dream of...

BECKHAM. No really, I never actually sleep in hotels anyway.

CAMERON. Why not?

BECKHAM. I think it's the pillows. I just like my own pillow. And to be honest I can't sleep unless I've had sex.

PENNY. Oh golly!

CAMERON. Oh dear. Not ever.

BECKHAM. Not really, no.

PENNY. Poor you!

BECKHAM. Yeah.

CAMERON. Another reason for not sharing a room with you. Look, Penny, why don't you come back and tell me when my shower is working and when my room is free of all Portuguesers and then perhaps I can move in. Don't be afraid to assert yourself.

PENNY. Right.

ASHOK *arrives carrying a tray of crisps, etc.*

(*To* WILLIAM.) Lovely to meet you anyway.

ASHOK. Pringles, crisps, pork scratchings and one pot of tea.

PENNY *leaves.*

CAMERON. Perfect. Thank you very much.

ASHOK. May I just take this opportunity to say that I thought what the Russian delegation said about your capital city was a disgrace.

WILLIAM. What did they say?

ASHOK. They referred to it as a centre of 'violence and alcoholism'.

WILLIAM. That's a bit harsh.

CAMERON. Coming from a Russian.

ASHOK. Of course there have been occasional incidents of fighting and drinking amongst the uneducated classes, the hoi polloi if you like, in such towns as Newcastle and Birmingham, but to tar everyone with the same feather is unforgiveable. Now, I will leave you gentlemen to it but I am standing directly outside your door. Just say my name and I am at your disposal.

CAMERON. Great, thank you very much, Ashok.

ASHOK *goes out*.

So. My God is that the time. Right. Onwards and hopefully upwards. Lobbying tactics. The state of play as far as I can see is as follows: the Russians are the hot favourites followed closely by two other teams, basically the Iberians.

BECKHAM. The who?

CAMERON. The Iberians. The Spanish and Portuguese.

BECKHAM. *Three* teams.

CAMERON. No just the two. The Iberians.

BECKHAM. *One* team.

WILLIAM. The Iberians *are* the Spanish and the Portuguese.

CAMERON. Yes.

BECKHAM. Oh right.

CAMERON. Okay? And in order to go through to the next round of voting, from our final presentation, at eleven o'clock tomorrow morning incidentally, realistically we need to secure a minimum of seven votes, six in effect as we already have one from our own man. Now…

BECKHAM. That's the same as the airline.

WILLIAM. What?

BECKHAM. Iberia.

WILLIAM. Yah I think it is.

CAMERON. …as I understand it we have three meetings of immediate concern. William, you're seeing Jack Warner later on this evening who effectively is worth three votes to us. To kick off so to speak what is it that you're going to impress upon him that makes England such a strong contender. Other than the fact that we bought his wife a very expensive handbag?

BECKHAM. A handbag?

CAMERON. Yes.

BECKHAM. A handbag!

CAMERON. Burberry, yes.

BECKHAM. What did we do that for?

CAMERON. Hopefully we'll find that out tomorrow.

WILLIAM. Getting back to the question I think if you look at the technical aspects alone England really does have a fantastic bid. Added to which we have some of the best facilities in the world, we have a first-class transport network, and without doubt we have some of the best iconic stadia already built ready and waiting... Lord's, The Oval, Edgbaston... I mean, these really are top-class grounds that would be the envy of just about...

CAMERON. Just a... can I just stop you there for a second.

WILLIAM. Sure.

CAMERON. You mentioned the... that was all fine... but you mentioned the 'stadia'. Lord's, The Oval, et cetera.

WILLIAM. Yah?

CAMERON. You are aware that those are cricket grounds?

WILLIAM. Well yes, obviously.

CAMERON *and* BECKHAM *frozen to the spot.*

CAMERON. How much do you actually know about the World Cup 2018?

WILLIAM. How do you mean? I mean, I know it's for 2018 obviously and, well, yah it's the World Cup, I'm not quite sure what you're getting at?

BECKHAM. It's football.

WILLIAM. Football! I thought...

BECKHAM *and* CAMERON *freeze.* WILLIAM *suddenly laughs. They realise he is joking.*

Sorry. Sorry. I couldn't resist. It was actually Dad's idea and I promised I'd give it a go.

CAMERON. Very good, very good. No, you certainly had me.

BECKHAM. You had me too.

WILLIAM. Sorry.

CAMERON. Good old Dad. Yes, please do not do that again. Pause. Rewind. Where are we, other than even more short of time.

WILLIAM. Sorry, sorry. So what am I actually going to say to him… (*Beat*.) I suppose something along the lines of, you know, 'England is the motherland of football. The game was practically invented on our shores. And…'

CAMERON. Except it wasn't.

WILLIAM. Oh right.

BECKHAM. What?

CAMERON. Unfortunately.

BECKHAM. Football wasn't invented in England?

CAMERON. No.

BECKHAM. Where was it invented then?

CAMERON. China apparently.

BECKHAM. China! That can't be right.

CAMERON. Why not?

BECKHAM. Have you seen the Chinese play football? They're diabolical. That can't be right.

CAMERON. Yes, I wonder, changing tack slightly, whether it might be worth gently reminding Mr Warner that following on from his trip to Trinidad, David is proposing to open a number of his football academies across the Caribbean. You see I think this is where we can really score. Because we have opened our arms to people across the world, our country is culturally so rich and so diverse that we can produce a home crowd for every game. We can bring communities together and make it a truly global event, et cetera et cetera. Yes?

WILLIAM. Absolutely.

CAMERON. Excellent. David, first off you're seeing Mohamed Bin Hammam who is central to the Spain–Qatar voting alliance, which we really need…

BECKHAM. Sorry to interrupt but, I meant to ask… how exactly do you say his name?

CAMERON. Mohamed Bin Hammam.

BECKHAM. Mohamed.

CAMERON. Yes… Bin.

BECKHAM. Bin.

CAMERON. Hammam.

BECKHAM. Hamm…

CAMERON. Hammam.

BECKHAM. Hamm… am.

CAMERON. That's it. Mohamed Bin Hammam.

BECKHAM. Mohamed Ham…

WILLIAM. No, Bin.

BECKHAM. Bin.

WILLIAM. Hammam.

CAMERON. Mohamed Bin Hammam.

BECKHAM. Mohamed Ham Bimman… oh, sod it.

CAMERON. You know what, let's not get bogged down with… with details. What about the bullet points. Very often a personal story is a good way of getting people on side. I mean, you have a long relationship with the game. Is there a person or even better a story that you could tell somehow…

BECKHAM. Yeah, well a year ago my granddad died...

CAMERON. Good, very good.

BECKHAM. And it was my granddad Joe who took me to my first ever football match. He was a massive Tottenham Hotspur fan and obviously I'll never forget how proud he was when I first signed up for the Bobby Charlton Sports Academy and, soon after I started there I realised... I said to myself, 'David, you've got two alternatives, you can either play football and go wherever that takes you or you can go to school and get some qualifications.'

WILLIAM. That's actually... sorry to stop you... that's actually only one alternative.

BECKHAM. You can either play football *or* you can go to school and get some qualifications.

WILLIAM. Yah. But if you're actually going to say that, it is only one alternative.

CAMERON. He is right, perhaps it would be better if...

BECKHAM. Wait a minute... wait a minute. *Either* football, yeah... *or* school. That's a choice, right?

CAMERON. *A* choice. Right.

BECKHAM. Between two different things?

CAMERON. Yes.

BECKHAM. So. Two alternatives.

CAMERON. Er no, but look, it really doesn't matter.

BECKHAM. How do you mean 'no'? Football, one alternative, school another, I think you'll find that makes two!

CAMERON. Weirdly, it doesn't.

BECKHAM. What!

CAMERON. But look, never mind, it doesn't matter and sadly we've run out of time, I think we'd better just concentrate on getting to our respective meetings and report back at around nine o'clock, does that sound okay?

WILLIAM. Very good.

CAMERON. By which time I might even have my very own room.

WILLIAM. Sorry, I didn't mean to...

CAMERON. It's not a problem, really. Okay, David?

BECKHAM. Not really. It's like you're telling me one and one don't make two...

WILLIAM. They do.

CAMERON. It's fine really it's fine.

BECKHAM. I mean, I don't mean to get the hump but people are always, you know, having a pop at me because I'm stupid, least that's what they say and yeah I do say some stupid things and obviously I have *done* my fair share of stupid things, but actually I do think about stuff quite a lot, more than people give me credit, and just cos you say and do stupid things doesn't necessarily mean you actually *are* stupid, does it?

CAMERON. Er...

WILLIAM. Who doesn't say stupid things?

BECKHAM. Exactly. I bet you've said some stupid things in your time.

WILLIAM. Oh God yah absolutely, almost certainly.

BECKHAM. Maybe not you that much cos you're the Prime Minister.

CAMERON. The trick is not to do it when there's a journalist around.

BECKHAM. It's not really fair though, is it.

CAMERON. Listen, David, let's put our cards on the table here, the fact is we are all successful men, however we got there, you with your extraordinary footballing talent and flair for fashion, me though I say it myself, blessed with a brain, a sense of leadership, vision and an ability I hope to communicate, and, William, you with... you with...

BECKHAM. His family.

CAMERON. Your family, exactly, but I'm afraid, this being England nobody likes success.

BECKHAM. Switzerland. This is Switzerland.

CAMERON. Yes but…

BECKHAM. That's what I mean, see? Everyone says stupid things…

CAMERON.…the point I'm trying to make is that because in England, and I know we're in Switzerland right now, David… here, but in England, were we there, nobody likes success which means that each of us in our different ways comes in for a lot of stick, it's the politics of envy, and you know what, the best thing you can do is just rise above it. Okay?

BECKHAM. Yeah.

WILLIAM. Defo.

CAMERON. Jolly good. Ashok!

ASHOK *enters instantly.*

ASHOK. Mr Cameron, sir.

CAMERON. We're off to our first round of meetings, I wonder if we could organise something a bit more substantial to eat for later on.

ASHOK. Of course, sir. 'No man can be a patriot on an empty stomach.' William Cowper, 1731 to 1800. What would you say if you were to return from your meeting and find a plate full to the brim with roast beef and crisp Yorkshire pudding?

CAMERON. Well…

ASHOK. Green peas, carrots and lashings of good, thick, brown gravy, followed by a tasty bowl of Eton Mess. Be honest now, sir, would not that fit the ticket?

CAMERON. Speaking for myself it most certainly would.

WILLIAM. Perfect.

BECKHAM. Go for it, yeah.

ASHOK. Excellent, excellent. And may I take this opportunity to wish you all the very best of luck.

CAMERON. Thank you.

ASHOK *leaves*.

Okay, so all looking good. Give it your best shot and see you all in a couple of hours for a debrief.

*They all make for the door.* BECKHAM *briefly checking himself in the mirror. The others wait.*

BECKHAM. It's funny how we always say 'green' peas, isn't it. Like as *if* we might get blue peas or red peas. But we never say orange carrots or, you know... purple beetroots...

CAMERON. Stay focused, guys.

BECKHAM. Or yellow custard.

*They exit.*

*Blackout.*

**Scene Two**

*We are now in* WILLIAM*'s suite. The living room. Identical design and decor to* BECKHAM*'s, only larger and plusher.* WILLIAM *is on the phone. A football sits on a chair.*

WILLIAM (*on phone*). Oh, not too bad. There's a really nice place just round the corner which you can see from the window but unfortunately we're not staying there. (*Beat.*) I don't know, I think it's something to do with the economy? (*Beat.*) No, I know but it's only a couple of nights tops. By the way, I was wondering if we should invite David and Victoria to the wedding… that would be good, wouldn't it, to have a few… ordinary people. (*Beat.*) You've had what?… A few thoughts. Great. Go on then, fire away. (*Beat.*) When you say a small affair, how small were you thinking? (*Beat.*) Right. Between fifty and a hundred… um… I'm not sure that's going to be possible. I mean, if you're going to be in the Abbey you really need to fill it. (*Beat.*) Oh right, blow out the Abbey altogether and… (*Beat.*) A field? What like a… What do you mean a field? (*Beat.*) Yah, that is quite a rethink, only Dad's quite traditional that way – (*Beat.*) Well again, white is traditional, maybe we should talk about this when I get back. Either way it's okay for me to ask David and Victoria, I mean, what if she wants to sing or something.

*The sound of manic shouting through the phone.* WILLIAM *has to hold it away from his head.*

Kate… Kate… are you alright? It's okay… chill. I said 'what if…'

*There is a knock at the door. The shouting continues nonstop.*

(*Calling.*) I'll be with you in a second! (*To* KATE.) Listen, calm down, I have to go, I'll call you later…

*He goes over and opens the door.* CAMERON *is there.*

CAMERON. Sorry, am I interrupting?

WILLIAM. No no, not at all, come in. Just… catching up with Kate.

CAMERON *enters, looking around.*

CAMERON. Very nice. Very nice indeed. I'm obviously in the wrong job. No sign of David yet?

WILLIAM. No, not yet.

CAMERON. Right. Well, we'd better wait for him before we… sort out the abracadabra.

WILLIAM. Oh my God. I haven't heard that for a while.

CAMERON. I bet. You were at Manor, weren't you?

WILLIAM. Yah. You?

CAMERON. JF. Wet-bob?

WILLIAM. You bet. You?

CAMERON. 'Fraid not.

WILLIAM. Too busy with the whacky baccy.

CAMERON. Steady. Too busy with the Georgics certainly. (*Laughs.*) Happy days.

WILLIAM. Happy days.

CAMERON. You know what?

WILLIAM. What?

CAMERON. All things considered I think it's going rather well.

WILLIAM. Really?

CAMERON. I mean, I've just come back from a terrifically good meet with Sepp Blatter. He's by and large very understanding about the whole *Panorama* stuff and altogether very supportive of our bid. He actually said to me that we have 'nothing to fear'. I think the key thing is to break the Spanish–Qatar voting alliance, if we can somehow drive a wedge between…

*Urgent knocking at the door*

WILLIAM/CAMERON. Come in! / Hello.

CAMERON. Sorry.

   BECKHAM *enters*.

BECKHAM. Guess what.

CAMERON. What?

BECKHAM. Palin's pulled out.

CAMERON. Pulled out of what?

BECKHAM. Coming here!

CAMERON. Sarah Palin?

BECKHAM. Yes! The Yanks aren't going to be too happy, are they.

CAMERON. Are you sure?

BECKHAM. They're all talking about it downstairs.

WILLIAM. Sarah Palin?

BECKHAM. Yes!

   *Silence. Suddenly* BECKHAM *walks out of the room.*

CAMERON. Is he alright?

WILLIAM. I didn't even know Sarah Palin was part of the American Bid Team.

CAMERON. Neither did I. Between you and me, I don't think it'll do them too much damage. Excuse me a second.

   *He takes out his phone, which is ringing.*

   (*On phone*.) Hello? (*Beat*.) Yes, just about. (*Beat*.) Oh Lord, you're joking. (*Beat*.) They've not even taken off yet? (*Beat*.) Well, she's coping if not exactly excelling. (*Beat*.) Yes, well, keep in touch.

   *The call ends.* BECKHAM *walks straight back in.*

BECKHAM. Sorry. Putin. Not Palin, Putin.

CAMERON. Putin! Are you sure?

BECKHAM. Positive. Putin's pulled out.

CAMERON. Well, that's great news! If Putin can't be arsed to turn up then that means either that he's given up or else that he's simply too bloody arrogant.

BECKHAM. Either way I don't think FIFA are going to be very impressed.

CAMERON. No, quite rightly. Very Russian.

BECKHAM. Did you ever see those pictures of him on horseback a couple of years ago, crossing the river.

CAMERON. Oh God, yes. Macho nonsense.

WILLIAM. I thought it was rather *Brokeback Mountain*.

BECKHAM. Rather what?

WILLIAM. The film about gay cowboys?

BECKHAM. Gay cowboys?

WILLIAM. Yah. Rather good actually.

BECKHAM. Yeah? Right.

*Knocking on the door.*

WILLIAM/CAMERON. Come in. / Hello.

CAMERON. Sorry.

ASHOK *enters.*

ASHOK. Excuse me, sirs. I thought you would like to know that the Ladbrokes have shortened the odds on England from three to one to thirteen to eight.

WILLIAM. Really!

CAMERON. This is all good stuff.

ASHOK. I feel a seismic shift, sir, a seismic shift.

CAMERON. I don't know about seismic but it's very good news.

ASHOK. You know what springs to mind, sir? The year 1879...
the battle of Rorke's Drift, when one hundred and fifty
British soldiers armed only with the humble Martini-Henry
rifle, their backs to the wall, fought off over four thousand
Zulus intent on their destruction as Zulus unfortunately so
often are. History repeats itself in unexpected ways.

CAMERON. I think you're being a little bit optimistic there...

ASHOK. Now, sir, let me chase up the roast beef.

ASHOK *exits*.

BECKHAM. He's got a point.

CAMERON. Indeed. So how did the meetings go? William,
how was Warner?

WILLIAM. Fantastic. Very warm, very friendly. He did talk
about the marriage.

CAMERON. Your marriage?

WILLIAM. Yes. He said... he said that marriage was a bit like a
football match, to win you have to be determined and
prepared to change your tactics. Or something like that.

CAMERON. Right.

WILLIAM. I just wondered afterwards whether it was like a
coded message and that he was saying that we should change
*our* tactics for the bid, I don't know.

CAMERON. No, sounds to me like you were bonding, which is
good. What do you think, David?

BECKHAM. 'Marriage is like a football match'?

CAMERON. Yes.

BECKHAM. I don't think so.

CAMERON. I suppose what he meant was...

BECKHAM. For a start, football is played on a big grass...

CAMERON. No, well, let's not get bogged down with that. You felt it was a good meeting.

WILLIAM. Defo.

CAMERON. Excellent. David, Mohamed Bin Hammam. How did you get on?

BECKHAM. Very good. Very, you know, positive. He's a very nice man. He was wearing a really nice linen top with slightly flared sleeves. What did we talk about? Er… well, we talked about that for a bit. What else? Oh, in the end I just called him Bin.

CAMERON. Bin.

BECKHAM. Yeah. Just to be on the safe side.

CAMERON. Right.

BECKHAM. We did talk about football. And yeah, at the end of the day it all went very well, I'd say I was about eighty, eighty-one per cent certain of his vote.

CAMERON. Great. Good. Dare I say it but there are signs, very definite signs that we could turn this thing around and that didn't appear to be too much of a possibility this time yesterday so… well done all round, guys.

*A knock on the door.*

WILLIAM/CAMERON. Yes? / Hello?

CAMERON. Sorry.

PENNY *enters.*

PENNY. Hello again, everyone. Sorry to interrupt.

CAMERON. Shower fixed, I hope?

PENNY. Yes!

CAMERON. Excellent. And not a Portugueser in sight.

PENNY. No! Not a…

CAMERON. Excellent. So I can move in… when?

PENNY. Well, in theory…

CAMERON. No. No, I don't want theory. I want a time. Simple as that.

PENNY. Yes, no, I do understand. The thing is there was a bit of a misunderstanding on the desk and… to cut a long story short… as soon as the shower was fixed, an Australian gentleman checked into the room.

CAMERON. An Australian gentleman.

PENNY. Yes.

CAMERON. That also is a contradiction in terms. What Australian gentleman?

PENNY. Well, it's a bit complicated but…

CAMERON. No, Penny, it's not complicated. It's not complicated at all. I am here on official business. We are *all* here on official business. I am the Prime Minister of England, for God's sake, just get me in that room!

*The room phone rings.* WILLIAM *answers.*

WILLIAM (*on phone*). Hello.

CAMERON (*to* PENNY). Sometimes you just have to go the extra mile.

WILLIAM. Yah, he is. Hold on a second. (*To* CAMERON.) It's for you.

CAMERON. Who is it?

WILLIAM (*on phone*). Who is it, please? (*To* CAMERON.) It's Nick.

CAMERON. Nick who?

WILLIAM (*about to ask but the person on the other end has heard*). Nick Clegg.

CAMERON. Oh God. Could you tell him… no, I suppose I'd better…

*He goes over to the phone.*

Nick, hello look, is it urgent?

BECKHAM (*to* PENNY). Don't worry, it'll get sorted.

PENNY. Hope so.

BECKHAM. Course it will. He can sleep in my bed and I'll sleep in yours.

*He winks at her.* PENNY *nervous, excited laughter.*

(*To* WILLIAM.) So how many people are you expecting for the wedding?

WILLIAM. Oh God, I don't know. Don't suppose there'll be any problem shifting tickets though.

BECKHAM. You're selling tickets?

WILLIAM. No, no, not literally.

BECKHAM. Cos if you were, I'd take a couple.

PENNY. Golly, so would I!

WILLIAM (*laughing*). Right, no.

CAMERON (*on phone*). The BSkyB bid is not something I intend to get involved in and nor should I.

BECKHAM. You could have the reception at Wembley.

WILLIAM. Right.

BECKHAM. There's a few people I could have a word with. Plenty of space. And they'd take the posts down.

CAMERON (*on phone*). I think I've made my position on this quite clear already…

WILLIAM. Yah. No, I think we'll stick to the Palace. But listen, I meant to say earlier Kate and I would love it if you and Victoria could come along.

CAMERON (*on phone*). Definitely, yes.

BECKHAM. Oh really? That's fantastic. She'll be well chuffed. I know that for a fact. As a matter of fact… I shouldn't really be telling you this… but there's a little number she's been working on ever since she found out you was engaged.

PENNY. Oh wow!

BECKHAM. I don't want to give too much away but if you could set aside five, ten minutes tops in the Abbey, maybe towards the end. Could, you know... put the icing on the cake so to speak.

PENNY. How exciting!

WILLIAM. Yah. Yah. Let me get back to you on that.

CAMERON (*on phone*). Nick... Nick, listen to me...

BECKHAM. Also, I've got to say something now, I might be out of order and if I am I apologise... don't... cut me head off or whatever... but what with you getting married in a couple of months but more immediate with the presentation tomorrow and wanting to get everything, you know, spot on and that, I couldn't help noticing but you've got quite a flaky scalp.

WILLIAM. Oh right.

BECKHAM (*to* PENNY). Hasn't he?

PENNY. Er...

BECKHAM. You don't mind my...

WILLIAM. No, no God, no.

CAMERON (*on phone*)....no, you may not, I will definitely be back in time, got to run, sorry. Bye.

BECKHAM. Is that like a regular thing or...

WILLIAM. Well, kind of, yeah.

CAMERON. Right. Penny. (*Takes her to one side.*) You have a very impressive CV but when all is said and done, a CV is only a piece of paper. If you can't organise something as basic as a room then your chances...

PENNY. Oh, I can!

CAMERON. Then in God's name do it!

PENNY. Right.

CAMERON. Less 'golly' and more guts.

PENNY. Leave it with me.

PENNY *goes to the room phone and makes a call.*

WILLIAM. I do use a dedicated anti-dandruff lotion.

BECKHAM. You what!

WILLIAM. What?

BECKHAM. Anti-dandruff lotion! Do you realise what you're doing?

WILLIAM. How do you mean?

CAMERON. Chaps…

BECKHAM. You might as well be using weedkiller. No wonder you're losing your hair. What about conditioner?

WILLIAM. Oh yes.

BECKHAM. Every time?

WILLIAM. Probably not.

CAMERON. Chaps…

BECKHAM. That is your biggest mistake. Shampoo, condition. Shampoo, condition. Left foot, right foot, every time I'm telling you.

CAMERON. Chaps, sorry to interrupt but can we… we're in danger of losing focus here a little. Dare I say it but…

BECKHAM. Seriously…

CAMERON. By my calculations anyway I rather think we've increased our share of the vote from one to precisely four or maybe even five. And that's *before* the roast beef so onwards and upwards. Penny?

PENNY. They're getting back to me.

CAMERON. Right. Well, stay here and if they haven't got back to you in five minutes, I want to see you getting back to them. Next up, William, I gather you're seeing Worawi Makudi from Thailand, and David you're due to see Leoz from Paraguay. Any thoughts about how to approach them?

BECKHAM. No room for complacency.

CAMERON. Absolutely not.

BECKHAM. Against France in '96 we was three nil up...

CAMERON. David, I'm just acutely aware of the time...

BECKHAM. No worries.

CAMERON....but yes, no complacency. We have a good bid, we have a great bid. Why? Because we have the venues, the facilities, the transport networks and above all we have the enthusiasm for football... all of which put together will guarantee an absolutely first-class World Cup.

*A knock on the door.* WILLIAM *opens it to* ASHOK, *who wheels in a tray covered with silverware/food.*

ASHOK. Roast beef and Yorkshire pudding. I can only apologise that it has come to you so late, the reason being that I insisted, sir, that it was a British cow and I'm glad, sir, that I did because the first cow they sent me was from France and I think I'm right in saying, sir, you are not a fan of the French.

CAMERON. Well, who is?

*Laughter.*

ASHOK. 'Who is.' Very good, sir. Very humorous. Anyhow, I put my foot down, right down, and demanded that a British cow be drummed up by hook or by crook and by heaven it was.

CAMERON. Thank you very much.

BECKHAM. I'm starving.

WILLIAM. I could eat a horse.

ASHOK. Horse? You want horse?

WILLIAM. No, no...

ASHOK. If you're not happy with the roast beef, I can you get you horse.

WILLIAM. No really, roast beef is exactly what I'm after.

ASHOK. Very good. My favourite. Please, carry on. I'll be two ticks.

CAMERON. Penny, five minutes is up. Off you go.

PENNY (*looking at her watch*). I make it only…

CAMERON. No arguing. Get stuck in.

> PENNY *leaves*. ASHOK *busies himself getting a table out into the middle of the room, setting the chairs round it, setting the tableware and food, etc.*

> So, chaps, the only other thing that you might touch on is the issue of legacy. And this is somewhere where I believe we really can deliver. After all, it's not as if we're having to build a whole load of stadiums that…

WILLIAM. Stadia.

CAMERON. What?

WILLIAM. Stadia.

CAMERON. Yup. Quite right, stadia. Sorry, I've completely lost my thread…

WILLIAM. Oh sorry, that's my fault.

CAMERON. No, quite right, the devil is in the detail. Ah yes, we want to ensure that football is played in our stadia in 2018 and beyond.

ASHOK. Forgive me for interrupting you, sir… dinner is served.

CAMERON. Oh, look at that. You've done us proud, Ashok. If you ever want a job at Number 10…

WILLIAM. Or the Palace…

ASHOK. Please enjoy your food before it gets cold and if there's anything, God forbid, that I have forgotten, remember I am just outside your door.

CAMERON. Wait a second. Not before we've drunk a toast. Grab your tea, everyone. I should like to propose a toast to Ashok.

ASHOK. To me! Oh my goodness.

CAMERON. His diligence, his good nature, and his loyalty.

ALL. To Ashok.

WILLIAM (*joking*). Speech!

*They laugh and are about to sit down to eat when* ASHOK *starts.*

ASHOK. In the winter of nineteen hundred and eight-eight, on the fifteenth of February, in Bombay, a test match took place between India and England. It is a match that is remarkable for a variety of reasons. For one, Ian Botham, that giant of English cricket, takes no less than ten wickets, a new world record. For two, his wicketkeeper Bob Taylor takes no less than nine catches. For three, the same Bob Taylor goes on to share a sixth wicket stand with Ian Botham worth one hundred and seventy-one runs, a new record against India… but the real reason this match comes to mind is because halfway through his innings Bob Taylor much to his dismay was deemed to be Leg Before Wicket by the umpire and was just beginning his return journey to the pavilion when the Indian captain, Gundappa Viswanath, intervened, overruled the umpire and invited him to return to the crease. An invitation which Bob Taylor gratefully accepted and went on to score a match-winning forty-three runs, thus ensuring victory for the English team. And now I have a question for you. Who do you think enjoyed the best night's sleep that night? Ian Botham? Bob Taylor? Gundappa Viswanath? No. The answer, gentlemen… is me.

CAMERON. You! How come?

ASHOK. Because at the end of the match, as the Indian spectators went home, their tail between their legs, a seventeen-year-old boy ran on to the pitch and, before you could say Jack Robinson, picked up the match ball, stuffed it into his pocket and ran like billy-oh all the way home where he slept like a baby with the cricket ball tucked under his pillow.

WILLIAM. It was you.

ASHOK. It was me. And what I learned that day, apart from the importance of seizing the day, apart from the value of fair play, is that given a level playing field, the best team will win! Not only *will* they win, not only do they *deserve* to win, they have a *right* to win.

CAMERON. Bravo.

*They all applaud.*

ASHOK. To Bob Taylor.

ALL. To Bob Taylor.

ASHOK. To Ian Botham.

ALL. To Ian Botham.

ASHOK. And to England.

ALL. To England.

*He watches as they all drink. Blackout.*

## Scene Three

*The next morning.* CAMERON*'s hotel room. The living room. the same decor and design as the others, only smaller. A football lies on the carpet, and two large bottles of water are on the table.* CAMERON *stands in the middle of the room. He addresses the audience. He has been up virtually all night.*

CAMERON. Thank you for the privilege of allowing me to present to you today. Football is our national game. It's part of what defines us as a country. But football in England is all the more special because it's also an international game. We are privileged to have some of the best footballers from all over the world...

*A knock at the door and* PENNY *enters.*

PENNY. Sorry, am I...

CAMERON. Don't worry. Good morning.

PENNY. It's a fantastic morning. I've just had the best cup of coffee that I've ever had in my life!

CAMERON. Lucky you. I've had five rather nasty ones.

PENNY. Do you ever get that feeling when you get out of bed and you look out of the window at the blue sky and you just think everything is right with the world, like I am so lucky to be alive!

CAMERON. Actually as Prime Minister, that doesn't tend to happen that often.

PENNY. Oh, but it should!

CAMERON. Yes, you're right it should. If it works for Noddy then why not for all of us. You'll be relieved to hear that the rest of the team are airborne at last.

PENNY. Oh good. How's the room?

CAMERON. Fine, thank you. Almost worth the wait.

PENNY. Oh thank God for that. And the bed?

CAMERON. Single. But then I am only the PM. To be honest I didn't see an awful lot of it.

PENNY. Me neither. I mean… I saw *my* bed obviously.

CAMERON. I'm just going through the opening. If you want to sit over there…

PENNY. Would you like me to look in on David just in case he's like… overslept or…

CAMERON. No, what I'd like you to do is to pour three glasses of water and put them on the table there.

PENNY. Fine.

CAMERON. We are privileged to have some of the best footballers from all over the world playing week in, week out in our premier and football leagues. Players like Clint Dempsey, Brad Friedel, Marcus Ha… Hay…

PENNY. Hahnemann…

CAMERON. Hahnemann… Hahnemann… damn it. Why can't he have an ordinary name like… Smith… or Rowbottom…

PENNY. I think Hahnemann probably is quite an ordinary name…

CAMERON. Only if you happen to live in Oberammergau or wherever… Players like Marcus Hahnemann….

*A knock on the door.* WILLIAM *enters. His face/cheeks are massively swollen.*

Oh my God!

CAMERON. What the hell… what happened?

WILLIAM (*with difficulty*). I don't know, I cut myself shaving last night and when I got up this morning, it had just swollen up.

PENNY. Shall I get a doctor?

CAMERON. Are you in pain?

WILLIAM. No.

CAMERON. This is a disaster!

PENNY. It must have got infected.

CAMERON. A complete disaster! Let me have a closer look.

*WILLIAM approaches him. CAMERON examines his face.*

We are kiboshed. Completely kiboshed. Short of the Iberians going down with food poisoning and the Russian delegation being kidnapped overnight.

WILLIAM. Or me making a miraculous recovery!

*He removes wads of cotton wool from his mouth and beams at them both.*

CAMERON. What on earth! Oh, I see.

WILLIAM (*laughing*). Couldn't resist.

CAMERON. It was a joke.

WILLIAM. Sorry. I shouldn't have really.

CAMERON. No, no… that's… hilarious.

PENNY. You certainly fooled me.

CAMERON. Yes and me.

WILLIAM. You've got to see the funny side of life sometimes though, haven't you.

PENNY. Oh gosh, yes.

CAMERON. Difficult though that may be on occasions. Forget the coffee, I think I need a stiff whisky. And a baseball bat. No, that's me joking now. So when did you cook that up?

WILLIAM. Actually, it was during my meeting with Worawi Makudi last night.

CAMERON. *During* the meeting.

WILLIAM. My granddad did it to my gran once in Beijing, to get out of a state banquet.

PENNY. Golly.

WILLIAM. Not even as a joke.

PENNY. He must like really hate Chinese food.

WILLIAM. No, just the Chinese actually.

CAMERON. The meeting with Makudi?

WILLIAM. Went very well as a matter of fact.

CAMERON. Good.

WILLIAM. We talked about… football, obviously. And Thai food. Which funnily enough is one of my favourites. And yah, he said what a good bid it was and how he was right behind us so…

CAMERON. Fantastic.

WILLIAM. I mentioned the friendly, like we said, and he seemed quite happy. He said something about tickets for the Olympics.

CAMERON. Yes.

WILLIAM. The finals.

CAMERON. Okay.

WILLIAM. Oh, and accommodation for that fortnight.

CAMERON. Right.

WILLIAM. At The Dorchester.

CAMERON. Okay. I think we can live with that. I'll have a word with Boris.

WILLIAM. I wouldn't mind going through my contribution if that's okay.

CAMERON. Of course.

WILLIAM. Just to get in the mood. And there's a thought I had…

CAMERON. Before you do though… drink that.

*He passes him a glass of water that* PENNY *has poured.*

WILLIAM. I'm alright actually, I've just…

CAMERON. Trust me. Just do it. I'll explain later.

WILLIAM. Right. The whole lot.

CAMERON. The whole lot. Really.

WILLIAM *drinks it.*

Okay, all yours. Penny's our autocue. I'll be the panel. Okay? So here we are. We've had the intro, seen the video and… you're *on.*

WILLIAM. The English love football and that is why it would be such an honour for us to host the 2018 FIFA World Cup. But it's not just about us. I give you an assurance that England is committed to playing its full and proper role in… The thing that slightly worries me, particularly having heard David's bit as well… is that it is all a bit… serious… and I'm just wondering if I should work in a joke of some sort.

CAMERON. A joke?

WILLIAM. Yah.

CAMERON. What were you thinking of this time, a giant safety pin through your skull?

PENNY. Now *that* would be…

WILLIAM. Not that kind of thing, no.

PENNY. No.

CAMERON. It's not really a joky kind of event, is it.

WILLIAM. Oh God no, but you know sometimes humour can win people round as much as all the other stuff. Ask Kate.

*He laughs.*

CAMERON. Do we really want people laughing at us?

*A knock at the door.* CAMERON *opens to* BECKHAM.

Ah… we were beginning to worry.

BECKHAM. Have you seen this?

*He holds up a copy of the* Sun.

An open letter to FIFA on the front page. Fantastic. They're right behind us, the whole country's behind us. 'The Three Lions.'

CAMERON (*reading*). The three lions! I like it.

BECKHAM. Is there any coffee?

CAMERON. On its way. But while you're waiting…

*He passes him a glass of water.*

Get that down you.

BECKHAM. What's this about then?

CAMERON. This is a little known trick passed on from another great Tory, Enoch Powell… bit before your time, but every time he made a big speech, every time he made a major decision he made sure he did it with a full bladder. Why? Because it gave him focus. And we need focus. Sounds a bit odd I know but I've done this on a number of occasions and believe me it works so… get it down you.

BECKHAM. Give it a go.

*He drinks.*

WILLIAM. Sleep okay?

BECKHAM. Yeah. Like a log.

PENNY. Ooh. Lucky… someone.

*A smile between* BECKHAM *and* PENNY *that* CAMERON *intercepts.*

BECKHAM. The words was going round and round my head this morning though. I don't usually get nervous now before a big game. But this is different.

PENNY. Of course it is.

CAMERON. Right. Anyhow, D-day has arrived. The Dutch and the Belgians are doing their stuff as we speak, next up the Spanish and Portuguese, and then it's us. How did you get on with Nicolás last night?

BECKHAM. Who?

CAMERON. Nicolás Leoz from Paraguay.

BECKHAM. Oh Leoz, yeah pretty well. He was a little bit moody. (*Beat.*) Did you say Paraguay?

CAMERON. Yes.

BECKHAM. Right. (*Beat.*) That would explain it.

CAMERON. What?

BECKHAM. I thought it was Uruguay.

CAMERON. Oh dear.

PENNY. Only a couple of letters different.

BECKHAM. Yeah.

CAMERON. So what did you talk about?

BECKHAM. Uruguay. But it seemed to go alright.

WILLIAM. Did he say he'd vote for us?

BECKHAM. He didn't say he wouldn't.

CAMERON. Not quite the same, is it…

WILLIAM. I don't think it matters.

BECKHAM. How do you mean?

WILLIAM. I think we're there, aren't we? I think we're up to seven possibly even eight votes which'll take us through to the next round.

CAMERON. Provided we don't screw up on our final presentation.

*He pours them both more water.*

WILLIAM. More! God. So what do *you* think about maybe introducing some humour into...

CAMERON. Yes, William was just saying that he felt we needed to lighten the presentation just a little. Maybe by way of a joke. My view is that...

WILLIAM. I did actually have something in mind, I don't know if it's worth running it by you.

CAMERON. Feel free, but before you do... down the hatch.

*They drink.*

WILLIAM. Okay. Well, what I thought was... when I got to the bit about England organising big events and like how good we are at it, I could add on 'I know that we can deliver extraordinary public occasions and celebrations. I certainly hope so as I'm planning quite a big one myself next year.'

PENNY *laughs.* CAMERON *humours him and* BECKHAM *is silent.*

PENNY. Oh, that's very funny.

CAMERON. Penny, could you chase up the coffees?

PENNY. Of course.

PENNY *leaves the room.*

WILLIAM. What do you think?

CAMERON. I think it's...

BECKHAM. I don't get it.

CAMERON. Ah.

BECKHAM. Say it again, will you.

WILLIAM. 'I know that we can deliver extraordinary public occasions and celebrations. I certainly hope so as I'm planning quite a big one myself next year.'

*Pause.*

BECKHAM. No. Still don't get it.

WILLIAM. It's not really a 'getting' kind of joke.

BECKHAM. It's not really *any* kind of joke, is it.

WILLIAM. I probably didn't tell it right.

BECKHAM. If you said… 'I know that we can deliver, whatever it is, big public occasions and celebrations. I certainly hope so as I've got a big one myself.' That would be a joke. That would get a laugh. It would be a bit risky and I'm not saying you should…

CAMERON. Right. I'm stepping in here… David, if you don't mind I think I'm going to overrule you because, William, I think you were right first time. In the interests of time let's go with what you've got which is kind of funny without being funny if you know what I mean… which is a nice compromise.

*A knock on the door.* CAMERON *opens to let in* ASHOK, *carrying a tray of coffee.*

ASHOK. Thank you, sir. Good morning, Mr Beckham, sir, Your Royal Highness, I hope you are ready for your big day. I thought you would all like to know that as from this morning the Ladbrokes have made England *evens favourites* to win the bid, with Russian at six to five and Spain–Portugal trailing at six to one. And the bookies never get it wrong.

*They cheer.*

Coffee, sir?

BECKHAM. Please.

ASHOK *pours coffees.*

CAMERON. Gents, that's great news, but let's just keep our eye on the ball so to speak, what we need this morning is Oscar performances. It's all about focus. We have really got to be absolutely spot on. It only takes some little slip-up and the confidence goes, David, I'm sure you can talk about this better than I can…

BECKHAM. Yeah when we was playing…

CAMERON. But perhaps not now.

ASHOK. Anything else you require, sir?

CAMERON. No thank you, Ashok, you've done us proud.

ASHOK. Not at all, sir. When I return in a couple of hours I know in my heart of hearts that you will be the future hosts of the 2018 FIFA World Cup and I hope to be there on the day of the final at Wembley when once again England meet let us say their old foe Germany and in the dying seconds of that game, Mr Beckham, sir, you place the ball…

BECKHAM. Me? I don't think so.

ASHOK. Most certainly, sir, why not? Men play football well into their forties, Peter Shilton and Sir Stanley Matthews to name but two, why not you? Just imagine, sir, you place the ball five yards outside the penalty area and under the watchful eye of your Prime Minister and the heir to the British throne, you curl the ball with majesty and grace past a host of bamboozled krauts into the back of the net… don't tell me you have not dreamed of this moment.

BECKHAM. Well…

ASHOK. All of us. No? Come on, tell the truth.

CAMERON. Now you mention it…

*Laughter. They all concede.*

ASHOK. Of course. The best of British to all of you.

CAMERON. Thank you very much.

*He leaves.*

BECKHAM. I'd better get into training.

WILLIAM. It's not impossible, you know.

CAMERON. God no.

BECKHAM. Do you reckon? 2018. I'd be…

CAMERON. Anything and everything is possible.

WILLIAM*'s mobile phone rings.*

WILLIAM. Do you mind if I…?

CAMERON. Sure… just bear in mind we're on in less than half an hour.

WILLIAM (*on phone*). Hello, you.

WILLIAM *goes into the bedroom.* BECKHAM *concentrating.*

CAMERON. Everything okay?

BECKHAM. Forty-three.

CAMERON. Sorry?

BECKHAM. In 2018 I'll be forty-three.

CAMERON. Oh right.

BECKHAM. You never know.

*Pause.*

CAMERON. Nervous?

BECKHAM. A bit. No one *likes* getting older, do they.

CAMERON. Of the presentation I meant.

BECKHAM. Oh yeah. Definitely.

CAMERON. That's good. That's how it should be. Any final questions?

BECKHAM. No. (*Beat.*) Yeah actually… You don't happen to know whether he's got a corgi called Rex, do you?

CAMERON. A corgi called Rex?

BECKHAM. Yeah.

CAMERON. I've no idea. Why?

BECKHAM. Don't matter.

PENNY *enters.*

PENNY. Boris says he'll meet you after the presentation.

CAMERON. Right. Where is he?

PENNY. In the bar.

CAMERON. It's nine forty-five a.m.

PENNY. Yes.

CAMERON. Let's hope we win.

PENNY. Oh golly, yes.

CAMERON. If only for the barman's sake.

BECKHAM (*to* PENNY). Collar up or down?

PENNY. Oh goodness. Difficult one.

BECKHAM. Up's a bit more...

PENNY. Yes...

BECKHAM. But then down says something quite...

PENNY. It does, doesn't it... (*Beat*.) I think either way would be lovely...

BECKHAM. I'll leave it as it is.

WILLIAM *comes out of the bedroom.*

CAMERON. All set, everyone?

WILLIAM (*to* DAVID). Defo. By the way I just had a chat with Kate about the wedding... and the possibility of Victoria singing...

BECKHAM. Oh listen, I forgot to say... that's a freebie, that. It's on us.

WILLIAM. No...

BECKHAM. Yes really.

WILLIAM. No.

BECKHAM. I insist.

WILLIAM. Well, the thing is…

BECKHAM. Think of it as our wedding present.

CAMERON. Focus, everyone… final top-up…

*He refills their glasses.*

WILLIAM. I'm not sure if I can…

CAMERON. Last one. Just imagine it's best bitter.

WILLIAM. Ah, now you're talking…

BECKIIAM. If it's good enough for the Scouts, it's good enough for me.

CAMERON. Yes, that was Baden actually, not Enoch. Still… cheers, everyone!

*They all drink.*

Feel it yet?

BECKHAM. Yeah.

WILLIAM. Just a bit. I'm used to pints rather than gallons.

CAMERON. Concentrates the mind though, doesn't it…

WILLIAM. Yah.

CAMERON. Right!

PENNY. Good luck, all of you.

CAMERON. Let's… rock and roll.

BECKHAM. Rock and roll.

WILLIAM. Rock and roll.

PENNY. Rock and roll.

*They exit.*

**Scene Four**

CAMERON*'s hotel room. The bedroom door is open.* PENNY *waiting rather self-consciously. We and she hear the sound of seemingly endless peeing. It peters out… and then suddenly starts up again with renewed vigour.* CAMERON*'s phone rings.* PENNY *hesitates then answers.*

PENNY. Hello… (*Beat.*) No, this is Penny, I'm his PA. Well, I'm actually standing in for his PA as she got… (*Beat.*) He's rather tied up at the moment. (*Beat.*) Who? (*Beat.*) Right, well hang on, I'll see if he's finished. (*To* CAMERON.) David?

*There is no reply. She moves closer to the door.*

Prime Minister?

CAMERON (*off*). I won't be a second.

PENNY (*back on the phone*). He won't be long. (*Beat.*) Oh, it went very well, yes thanks so much for asking, it went *very* well indeed. (*Beat.*) Sorry, I can't… hello… hello?

*She puts the phone down as the peeing comes to an end. The toilet flushes and* CAMERON *comes out.*

CAMERON. Sorry about that. I wasn't bargaining on the presentation being delayed. Well, that went very well indeed!

PENNY. Good. Good. It certainly sounded… you know…

CAMERON. The presentation.

PENNY. Oh, I see. Yes it did, didn't it.

CAMERON. They were hanging on every word, every syllable as well they might. You have to savour these moments you know, Penny, they're few and far between. Did you speak to Boris?

PENNY. Sort of.

CAMERON. What did he think?

PENNY. He's gone back to the bar.

CAMERON. Oh no.

PENNY. And he's rather drunk.

CAMERON. For goodness' sake.

PENNY. Rebekah Brooks just called.

CAMERON. Oh yes, what did she want?

PENNY. She got cut off but I think she just wanted to know how it all went...

CAMERON. I hope you didn't tell her anything.

PENNY. No. Well, nothing... you know. I did say it went well.

CAMERON. Penny, rule number one. Never give a journalist *anything* for free. If you scratch their back, make damn sure they scratch yours. I'll call her back.

WILLIAM *and* ASHOK *come in.* WILLIAM*'s trousers are drenched. A moment of shock.*

ASHOK. Mr Cameron, sir...

CAMERON. William!

WILLIAM. I've had a bit of an accident, I'm afraid.

CAMERON *starts laughing.*

CAMERON. Very good.

PENNY. Oh, I see...

CAMERON. A joke too far perhaps.

PENNY. Very funny.

WILLIAM. What?

CAMERON. I think your judgement may have let you down on this one, William...

WILLIAM. No, I really have had an accident.

ASHOK. Mr Cameron, sir, it's all my fault.

WILLIAM. No it's not, it was the effing tap.

CAMERON. What tap?

ASHOK. His Royal Highness came into the cloakroom. When
he wanted to wash his hands, I turned on the tap for him and
up came the water... wsht! All over his trousers, sir.

CAMERON. Oh no.

WILLIAM. I need to get out of these, do you mind if I...

WILLIAM *walks into the bedroom.*

ASHOK. How can I have been so foolish, sir! To jeopardise
everything you have worked so hard for.

CAMERON. Listen, it could have happened to anyone. No one
else saw him, did they?

ASHOK. No, sir.

CAMERON. Good. We wouldn't want anyone getting hold of
the wrong end of the stick.

*Knocking on the door.*

Come in!

PENNY *opens the door.* BECKHAM *comes in.*

BECKHAM. I reckon we nicked it, I can't imagine anyone
topping that!

CAMERON. Fingers crossed.

BECKHAM. And you know what, that drinking thing, specially
after the delay, that worked a treat. I was so focused I was
like burning a hole in the autocue.

CAMERON. You absolutely were.

BECKHAM. Where's William?

PENNY. He's in the bathroom.

CAMERON. Yes, he's had a rather unfortunate accident.

BECKHAM. Yeah? I've got some aloe vera in my...

CAMERON. No, not that kind of accident.

BECKHAM. What then?

> WILLIAM *comes out of the bathroom carrying his wet trousers. He wears a towel.*

WILLIAM. I've borrowed your towel, I hope that's okay.

CAMERON. Of course.

WILLIAM. This is terribly embarrassing.

BECKHAM (*getting the wrong end of the stick*). Oh right.

ASHOK. For me too, sir.

CAMERON. Listen, it could have happened to any one of us.

BECKHAM. Yeah.

CAMERON. I trust you have another suit with you?

WILLIAM. I don't actually. Not even a pair of trousers apart from jeans.

CAMERON. Only the announcement is coming up in ten minutes so we do rather need to sort this out.

ASHOK. Take mine, please, take mine.

CAMERON. That's very kind of you but...

PENNY. We also need to clear the room.

CAMERON. Do we? Why?

BECKHAM. I've got a pair of Paul Smith's that would suit you. Or if you wanted something a bit more formal... when I say formal I don't mean like it's belted or...

CAMERON. David...

BECKHAM....but you're quite narrow in the hip so...

CAMERON. David, he just needs a pair of trousers, any pair.

BECKHAM. He's a lot longer in the leg than I am, I've got nothing that'll fit.

CAMERON. He cannot attend the press conference in his
    underpants!

BECKHAM. Alright, alright. I think everyone's getting a bit…
    you know.

    *Pause.*

CAMERON. Right. This is what's going to happen. Boris is in
    the bar, yes?

PENNY. As far as I know.

CAMERON. Go and ask him if he has a spare pair of trousers.

PENNY. And if he hasn't?

CAMERON. We'll cross that bridge as and when.

PENNY. But what if he…

CAMERON. Penny, just get a pair of trousers off Boris. For
    once, don't ask any questions, just go the extra mile.

PENNY. Right. Right.

    *She goes out determinedly.*

CAMERON. Just when we were really getting into our stride.

WILLIAM. I'm sorry.

ASHOK. You are blameless, sir, believe me, if I could turn the
    clock back.

CAMERON. Look, it's not anybody's fault. It could have
    happened to any one of us.

BECKHAM. Happened to me once. In front of a room full of
    people. *And…* worsest of all… I was wearing the full
    England strip.

WILLIAM. No…

BECKHAM. Yeah. Whoosh! (*Beat.*) I was only six.

ASHOK. May I make a suggestion, sir?

WILLIAM. Please do.

ASHOK. I take your damp trousers now, sir. I give them to my brother Vikram and get him to dry them while you are attending the ceremony.

CAMERON. Excellent idea.

ASHOK. That way you'll be right as rain for the press conference and your moment of glory.

WILLIAM. Thanks very much, that would be great.

ASHOK. It's the least I can do, sir. Leave it with me.

*He exits carrying* WILLIAM'*s trousers.*

CAMERON. Look, I know this might not feel like the best moment to say this, particularly for you, William, but let's hang on to the fact that the presentation went bloody well and we have every right to be very, very pleased with ourselves.

BECKHAM. Yeah…

WILLIAM. Hear, hear.

PENNY *bursts in carrying a pair of Boris's trousers. Her hair is all over the place and her make-up all smeared, buttons all undone, completely dishevelled and out of breath. She offers* WILLIAM *the trousers.*

CAMERON. You did it!

BECKHAM. Well done.

WILLIAM. Thanks.

*He takes the trousers and goes into the bedroom.*

CAMERON. Are you alright?

PENNY. Just about. He really is very drunk.

CAMERON. Good work, Penny, good work.

BECKHAM. What happened?

PENNY. He didn't actually have a spare pair.

BECKHAM. So what are those?

WILLIAM (*off*). Oh God.

PENNY. It was his idea! In fact he insisted. Only he passed out while he was taking them off. So I took over and just as I got them off he woke up again.

CAMERON. Oh Lord.

PENNY. I think he rather got the wrong idea.

CAMERON. Oh no. He didn't… you didn't…

PENNY. No!

CAMERON. There are extra miles and extra miles.

PENNY. Yes. I did get the impression it had been rather a long time.

CAMERON. Well done, Penny.

PENNY. Oh and they want you all back now.

CAMERON. Already? That's a good sign. A clear winner.

WILLIAM. Are these alright?

*He stands wearing Boris's trousers. Slightly short and baggy. They stare at him.*

PENNY. I'll check you out of the room.

CAMERON. Feels like I've only just checked in.

PENNY. That way you can go straight from the conference room to the press call to the airport.

CAMERON. Fine, whatever's easiest. I'm more or less packed. Are you not coming in with us then?

PENNY. Oh no. Too nervous.

CAMERON. Oh, come on.

PENNY. No really.

CAMERON. Suit yourself.

WILLIAM. Are you sure these look alright?

CAMERON. You know, William, I for one would stand stark
    bollock naked on that stage if it's England's name that's on
    that piece of paper when it comes out of the envelope.

WILLIAM. Right.

BECKHAM. Hopefully it won't come to that.

CAMERON. Alright, everyone? The moment of truth.

*He opens the door.*

Good luck, chaps!

BECKHAM. Into the lion's den.

WILLIAM. Roar!

CAMERON *is last to leave. He turns, a 'fingers crossed'
gesture to* PENNY *who responds in kind. They exit.* PENNY
*heaves a huge sigh and collapses into the armchair.*


**Scene Five**

*The back wall is filled with a large screen. Projected on to it is
footage of the actual announcement, with Sepp Blatter opening
the envelope and announcing the winner. We cut to the
disappointed reactions of our trio, but as* WILLIAM *turns his
back to us, we see he is wearing Boris's trousers. We follow*
WILLIAM *from behind, walking out of the main auditorium
and down an empty corridor. As he passes an open doorway, a
plump, blond, trouserless figure leaps out and rugby tackles him
to the ground.*

*The screen goes to black, the sound fades and the lights come
up on* CAMERON's *empty hotel room.* CAMERON *bursts in.
He is speechless with rage. He paces around for a moment.*

CAMERON. Ashok!

*Silence.*

Ashok?

*Silence.* CAMERON *goes to the door and opens it. No one is there.*

*He takes out his phone and dials. No answer... he waits for the answering-machine.*

Penny, where are you? Could you meet me...

*A flustered-looking* PENNY *emerges from the bedroom. She isn't wearing any shoes.*

Oh, there you are.

PENNY. What are you...?

CAMERON. Russia!

PENNY. Russia!

CAMERON. Yes, Russia! After everything we've had to put up with.

PENNY. That's awful.

CAMERON. I never thought I'd ever hear myself use this word but I feel absolutely gutted. Between you and me, the entire disreputable circus that calls itself FIFA should be strung up by their geriatric balls and waterboarded at hourly intervals.

PENNY. Would you like to go for a walk?

CAMERON. A walk?

PENNY. Some fresh air might... Or would you like some Bach's Remedy? I've got some in my room.

CAMERON. No. Jesus wept!

PENNY. I expect poor David did as well.

ASHOK *enters.*

ASHOK. Mr Cameron, sir, I don't know what to say. Has the world gone mad? What next? The Olympics in Afghanistan? It buggars my belief.

CAMERON. And Russia! God Almighty. A country of millionaire kleptomaniacs, why doesn't FIFA just hand over responsibility lock, stock and barrel to the Mafia and have done with it. These people are a disgrace to football, and the most humiliating thing of all is that this decision was probably made weeks, even months before!

ASHOK. You think so?

CAMERON. Without a shadow of a doubt. Why do you think Putin didn't bother to come?

ASHOK. Because he knew he had already won!

CAMERON. Exactly.

PENNY. That's so dishonest. That's cheating! And fifteen thousand pounds? That's an awful lot of money.

CAMERON. What?

PENNY. Isn't that what the bid cost?

CAMERON. Million. Fifteen *million* pounds.

PENNY. Surely not!

CAMERON. Somewhere in that region, yes.

PENNY. Fifteen *million*. Oh my... and you could have spent that on hospitals, couldn't you?

CAMERON. Yes.

ASHOK. Or schools.

CAMERON. Yes.

PENNY. Or bailing out banks.

CAMERON. Yes. No. Well...

PENNY. I can see why you're so angry now.

CAMERON. Yes.

*Pause.*

PENNY. I wasn't actually expecting you to return to your room.

CAMERON. No well, I'm afraid I couldn't face the press immediately.

PENNY. Are you sure you don't want some Bach's Remedy?

CAMERON. You know, I've thought long and hard about it and I've come to the conclusion that there is literally nothing whatsoever to like about Sepp Blatter. I would call him a complete and utter prick if it wasn't so insulting to complete and utter pricks. Even his *name* is ridiculous. Sepp! It's at least three consonants short of resembling any kind of human name whatsoever. And then just as you think you're over the worst comes Blatter. Like being hit in the face by a wet flannel. He actually put his arm around me and told me we had nothing to fear! Two votes. *Two!* And one of those from our own man! I can tell you one thing, Mr Blatter and co will not be getting free tickets to the Olympics, they will not be staying at The Dorchester, in fact I going to stick an ASBO on them that prevents them from getting to within five miles of The Dorchester, they can all go and stay in the sodding Travelodge!

CAMERON *suddenly notices* PENNY *is wearing no shoes.*

What were you doing in my bedroom?

PENNY *(shifty)*. Just making sure you'd packed everything.

CAMERON. Right. Have I?

PENNY. Yes.

CAMERON *(making to go in)*. I'd better just…

PENNY. It's all done. Really.

CAMERON. Right. Good.

*Pause.*

PENNY. Very disappointing.

CAMERON *(eyeing the bedroom with suspicion)*. Yes, isn't it. So where are David and William, do you think?

PENNY. No idea.

CAMERON. None whatsoever.

PENNY. No.

CAMERON. Seeking consolation no doubt.

*Pause. He scrutinises her.*

Are you aware that you're wearing no shoes?

PENNY. Yes. Yes, I must have... left them in the bedroom.

CAMERON. You always take your shoes off to pack, do you?

PENNY. Not... *always*, no.

*Urgent knocking on the door.*

CAMERON. Come in!

WILLIAM *bursts in, completely dishevelled and wearing no trousers.*

ASHOK. Oh my giddy aunt.

CAMERON. Not again. Dear God, please let this be a joke.

WILLIAM. I've just been debagged by Boris.

PENNY. What!

WILLIAM. He forcibly removed my trousers.

CAMERON. If that *is* a joke then it's in very poor taste. Boris?

WILLIAM. Yes.

CAMERON. Took off your trousers?

WILLIAM. Yes. Or to be fair, *his* trousers. He was very drunk. And angry.

PENNY. I think someone must have put something in his drink.

CAMERON. Did anyone see this?

WILLIAM. No.

CAMERON. You're quite sure...

WILLIAM. I came straight here.

PENNY. The press call is in five minutes.

CAMERON*'s mobile phone rings.*

CAMERON. Oh Lord. (*On phone*.) Hello?... (*Beat*.) Oh hello, Rebekah... yes, sorry about that, could you possibly hold on one second. (*To* ASHOK.) Right. Ashok...

ASHOK. Sir.

CAMERON. Where are William's own trousers?

ASHOK. Vikram has them, sir.

CAMERON. We need them back immediately, dry or not dry.

ASHOK. Of course, sir. (*Beat*.) If I can find them.

CAMERON. I thought you said Vikram had them.

ASHOK. Yes but he's gone home, sir. Dicky tummy.

CAMERON. Gone home!

ASHOK. Leave it to me, sir, I'll do my best.

*He exits.*

WILLIAM. I also need to get back to my room.

CAMERON. Fine.

WILLIAM. Now!

CAMERON. Right. (*Beat*.) Take my trousers. I'll have whatever David can offer. Penny, go and retrieve your shoes. Plus anything else you've left in there. (*On phone*.) Hello there – (*Beat*.) No, no problems at all. (*Beat*.) What can I say? Obviously we're enormously disappointed as are an awful lot of people back home...

*As he speaks,* PENNY *scuttles back into the bedroom, closing the door behind her. During the conversation* CAMERON *removes his own trousers and gives them to* WILLIAM *who puts them on. At the moment they are both trouserless,* PENNY *comes out fully dressed.*

...it was a good bid, as a matter of fact we were led to believe it was the best bid, so yes, as I say tremendously disappointed. I just feel terribly sorry for the working people of our country who are going to have to miss out on a wonderful opportunity. (*Beat*.) Fifteen million, yes, it is a lot of money but we certainly gave it our best shot and I think we've emerged with great dignity. (*Beat*.) I have never said that multiculturalism has failed or indeed that we are cutting funding for school sports. (*Beat*.) Well, alright, maybe I did use those words but nevertheless sometimes what you say is not… what you… what you mean, I'm afraid I have to go now, Rebekah. (*Beat*.) Thank you. What? (*Beat*.) Of course not, I've made no secret of the fact that I think that the *Panorama* programme was ill advised but no, BBC funding will not be affected in any way whatsoever. Goodbye.

*He puts the phone down. He is now trouserless.* WILLIAM *is wearing* CAMERON's *trousers.*

In your dreams!

PENNY. They were under the bed. My shoes.

CAMERON. Right.

WILLIAM. Does this look alright?

CAMERON. It's fine.

WILLIAM. Right. If I see David I'll…

CAMERON. You won't.

WILLIAM *leaves. The phone rings again.*

(*On phone*.) Hello? Speaking. (*Beat*.) What? No comment. How did you get this…

*He slams the phone down. The room phone rings immediately.*

Oh no. I want these screened.

*But* PENNY *has already answered.*

PENNY (*on phone*). Hello? (*Beat*.) Yes he is. Hang on a second. (*To* CAMERON.) It's Nick.

CAMERON. Nick who? Oh God, no please, not Clegg… not now I'm… tell him I'm… tell him…

PENNY. What?

CAMERON. To go away.

PENNY (*on phone*). Go away.

CAMERON. No, Penny!

PENNY. What?

CAMERON. Not like that! Christ!

PENNY. I'm sorry, it's all been a bit of a roller-coaster.

CAMERON. Yes, so I gather. A lot of ups and downs one way or another. Perhaps if one or two people had concentrated a little bit more on the task in hand, we might have had a better result.

PENNY. What do you mean?

*A noise from the bedroom.*

CAMERON. I think you know exactly what I mean.

*Beat.*

PENNY. Would you like me to finish up here while you go down for the press call?

CAMERON. Dressed like this?

PENNY. Or we could go and see if we can find David anywhere…

CAMERON. I've got a better idea, why don't we both just sit here and wait for him to turn up. Far more entertaining.

*He grabs a chair and pointedly sits in it facing his bedroom door.*

The trouble is, Penny, you can take the boy out of the working class but you can't take the working class out of the boy. Only a complete dimwit would think of jeopardising his entire future for the sake of a bit of rumpy pumpy with a glorified internee who has a grapefruit instead of a brain.

PENNY. That's unfair. I don't know what you mean.

CAMERON. Are you going to spill the beans or shall we just sit here and wait?

PENNY *is too upset to speak*

Right. Option two it is. You see, a man on the phone just now accused me of hating football, of being here just for show, and he could not have been more wrong. I love football. What I hate, with a vengeance, is everything else about football. And top of that list… above never being able to park on a Saturday afternoon, above the marauding bands of drunken, shaven-headed football fans chanting their tuneless gobbits of indecipherable filth… above the complete monopolisation of my television set by footballing prophets and pundits spouting their endless and intrinsically tedious drivel… above all these, what I hate most about football… are footballers. With their trophy wives and their chavvy children for whom ordinary names aren't quite good enough, with their precious look-at-me haircuts and their pitiful post-match grunts, struggling their way from one word to the next, single-handedly massacring any adverb foolish enough to come their way, one eye already set on their three-in-a-bed late-night frolics. All of which apparently entitles them to be paid more in two months than most people earn in a lifetime. And for what exactly? For splitting the atom? No. For finding the cure for cancer? No. For services to world peace? I think not. What then?

*He walks over to the bedroom door and shouts at it.*

FOR BEING GOOD AT KICKING A BALL, OF COURSE! IT SURE AS HELL ISN'T FOR KEEPING THEIR COCK IN THEIR TROUSERS, WHICH IS SOMETHING THEY SEEM TO BE PARTICULARLY BAD AT. IN FACT YOU MIGHT EVEN ARGUE THAT APART FROM BEING ABLE TO KICK A BALL AND SPIT SOMETIMES AT THE SAME TIME, IT'S ONE OF THEIR FEW DEFINING FEATURES!

*The bedroom door suddenly opens and* LACHLAN, *a large good-looking Australian man in his thirties, steps out. He wears no shirt and is doing up his trousers as he speaks.*

LACHLAN. What the fuck are you doing in my room?

*Pause.*

CAMERON. What? Penny... I'm...

PENNY. I didn't know what to do!

CAMERON. What is going on? Who are you?

LACHLAN. I'm Lachlan O'Riley.

CAMERON. Well, my name is David Cameron.

LACHLAN. I don't give a toss who you are, mate, I just want to know what the hell you are doing in my room.

CAMERON. I also happen to be the Prime Minister of England.

LACHLAN. Yeah right and I'm the Queen of fucking Sheba.

CAMERON. Penny...

PENNY. There was no room in the annexe.

*A knock at the door.* WILLIAM *and* BECKHAM *come in. They are talking animatedly, oblivious at first to the others.*

BECKHAM. I'm not saying it's not going to work, obviously David's inside leg is closer to mine than yours but...

LACHLAN. What is this, a bloody party? (*To* WILLIAM.) You look familiar, mate. We met before?

WILLIAM. No, I don't think so.

LACHLAN. You don't open the bowling for the Melbourne Anklebiters, do you?

WILLIAM. No.

LACHLAN. Jeez, you look familiar. What's your name?

*Beat.*

WILLIAM/BECKHAM. Steve. / Wazza.

*Pause.*

LACHLAN. Well which?

WILLIAM/BECKHAM. Wazza. / Steve.

LACHLAN. Right. I'll just let you get on with your identity crisis. (*To* BECKHAM.) Fuck me, I know who *you* are.

BECKHAM. Yeah?

LACHLAN. David Beckham, Jeez! Football. That's a shite game if ever there was one. Who wants to watch a bunch of millionaires with dodgy haircuts kicking a ball around. You're lucky I don't throw you out the room right now.

PENNY. He's a cricket fan.

LACHLAN. Too right I am.

CAMERON. Penny...

LACHLAN. You know what my old dad used to say? If cricket's a five-hour fuck on a four-poster bed with the three-times Miss South East Asia, football's more like a one-minute wank in the back of the car when your mum's driving. No hard feelings but he was right.

CAMERON (*to* PENNY). Could you please explain what is happening.

LACHLAN. She knocked on my door last night and told me she needed my room urgently. I told her to get stuffed. She begged me. I told her to get stuffed again. Then she started to get abusive which I quite liked. I offered her a drink, we started talking and one way and another we decided we quite fancied each other. Anyhow to cut a long and pretty filthy story short, I spent the night in her room on condition I could be back in here by three o'clock this afternoon.

PENNY. Three *thirty*.

LACHLAN. So at *three* o'clock I came back, she turned up five minutes later, only then we discovered we had a bit of unfinished business from last night. And here we all are.

CAMERON. Right. Okay, this is what's going to happen...

LACHLAN. No sorry, mate, I'll tell *you* what's going to happen... seeing as how I'm the one wearing the trousers.

I'm going out to buy a newspaper and by the time I come back I want you lot out of here or I call security.

CAMERON. Wait a second…

LACHLAN (*to* PENNY). You coming?

CAMERON. No she's not.

LACHLAN. I was speaking to her, mate, not you.

PENNY. No, I think I'd better…

LACHLAN. No worries. Nice meeting you all.

*He walks out of the room. Silence.*

CAMERON. Dear God. I have never been spoken to like that by *anyone*.

PENNY. I'm sorry.

CAMERON. Least of all by an Australian. (*To* PENNY.) Who is this man?

PENNY. His name is…

CAMERON. I know what his name is. What does he do?

PENNY. He's a milkman.

CAMERON. A what?

BECKHAM. Someone who delivers milk.

CAMERON. I do know what a milkman is, David.

BECKHAM. Right.

CAMERON. I wasn't aware they had milkmen in Australia.

WILLIAM. I didn't know they had milk.

BECKHAM. They've got sheep.

WILLIAM. Yah but milk comes from cows, so…

CAMERON. Could I be awfully rude and just ask both of you to be quiet for one second.

WILLIAM/BECKHAM. Sure. / Go ahead.

CAMERON. He's a milkman.

PENNY. Yes.

CAMERON. He told you that.

PENNY. Yes.

CAMERON. And what exactly makes you believe him?

PENNY. Why shouldn't I?

CAMERON. Did he by any chance ask you any questions?

PENNY. A few.

CAMERON. And a little alarm bell didn't go off at all? It didn't occur to you that something else might be going on?

PENNY. Such as what?

CAMERON. Such as that he might be lying and that he might be a journalist.

PENNY. Oh no, no he's not a journalist.

WILLIAM. How do you know?

PENNY. He told me he wasn't.

BECKHAM. Did he have any milk in his room?

CAMERON. FOR FUCK'S SAKE!

*He grabs hold of the football and thrusts it into* BECKHAM'*s hands.*

That's for you!

*He scrabbles around in his pocket and takes out a five-pound note and a Biro. He thrusts them into* WILLIAM'*s hands.*

And that is for you. Now. You play with the ball and *you…* colour in your grandmother's head… and both of you just SHUT THE FUCK UP UNTIL I HAVE FOUND OUT WHAT IS GOING ON!

*Silence. They all stare at him in disbelief.*

So. He *volunteered* that he wasn't a journalist.

PENNY. Yes.

CAMERON. Penny... if someone claiming not to be a journalist starts asking you questions, they most definitely will turn out to be a journalist.

PENNY. But that's lying!

CAMERON. Yes.

PENNY. Why would he do that?

CAMERON. Because he's a journalist! What exactly did you tell him?

PENNY. Nothing.

CAMERON. Oh, so you just slept with him and didn't say a word!

PENNY. He was nice to me.

CAMERON. Is that all it takes?

PENNY. It's a start.

CAMERON. I need to make a phone call. I also need some trousers. David...

BECKHAM. Right. Trousers. So what kind of look was you after?

CAMERON. The kind that stops me looking like a total twat will do very nicely!

BECKHAM (*making to leave*). Not sure I've got any of those...

CAMERON. No, no, I don't want either of you two leaving this room. It's not safe. Penny, take David's key.

*He notices she is crying.*

Penny, now come on. If it's any comfort I have a sneaking admiration for the lengths to which you were prepared to go to secure me a room.

PENNY. That's not why I did it!

CAMERON. But the fact is that in certain circles there is a minimum level of both decorum and discretion required.

BECKHAM (*to* WILLIAM). I had a wank in the back of a car once.

*They all look at him.*

CAMERON. What?

BECKHAM. I was just saying I did once have a wank – in the back of a Toyota Prius.

WILLIAM. Right.

BECKHAM. My mum wasn't driving. It was Gary Neville, as it happens. Even so… I wouldn't have done it otherwise. You wouldn't wank in the back of John Terry's Ferrari, would you?

WILLIAM. No I wouldn't.

BECKHAM. He'd go mental, I can tell you that for free. No, Wayne bet me five grand and I couldn't say no.

CAMERON. David, perhaps this is one best left for the autobiography.

BECKHAM. No, the thing is… it was good. And like, I know Gary's not my mum but when it comes to the difference between football and cricket that Aussie fella got it wrong.

CAMERON. Great. Glad we've settled that one. Penny, take David's key, go to his room and bring me back a suitable pair of trousers.

BECKHAM (*to* PENNY). The Armani, third from the left.

CAMERON. And try not to either talk or sleep with any journalists on your way.

*She goes out. Silence.*

I owe you both an apology. Penny's behaviour has been utterly reprehensible.

WILLIAM. Well, if you don't mind my saying, I don't think yours has been that great. I mean, you treat us like we're some kind of… of…

BECKHAM. Retards.

WILLIAM. Yah. I'm not just a pretty face, you know. I mean, I'm not even saying I *am* a pretty face. What I'm saying is that if I was, that wouldn't be *all* I was. I can actually do stuff, you know... I can fly a helicopter. Can you do that?

CAMERON. No I can't.

WILLIAM. Exactly. It's not easy. And there's other things... I can... I can... I'm all worked up now so I can't actually... think but... yah, I can definitely fly a helicopter. And I'm getting married.

CAMERON. William... both of you... I'm so sorry if I've upset you in any way whatsoever, you know I have the utmost respect for you as people and for the difficult jobs you do. So if I've been a bit tetchy in any way...

WILLIAM. Yah, you were a bit.

BECKHAM. I'd say more than tetchy.

WILLIAM. Shirty?

BECKHAM. I'd say ballistic.

CAMERON. Well, whatever word you eventually settle on, it was completely unacceptable and all I can say in my defence is that it's been a difficult day.

WILLIAM. Right.

CAMERON. *Mea culpa.* Now, if you'd just bear with me for one second...

CAMERON *takes out his phone.*

Rebekah Brooks, please. (*Beat.*) David Cameron. (*Beat.*) No, I know it's not a Tuesday but... (*Beat.*) Yes, I'm very busy too... (*Beat.*) Well, she was perfectly willing to speak to me a few minutes ago. (*Beat.*) Rebekah hi, sorry to drag you out of the hairdresser...

*He goes into the bedroom. Pause.*

BECKHAM. Well done, mate.

WILLIAM. Was that okay? I didn't go too far?

BECKHAM. No. He had it coming. Definite red card. All in all a bit of a downer though, isn't it. Russia.

WILLIAM. God yah. I was gutted when Blatter opened that envelope. Absolutely gutted. Weren't you?

BECKHAM. Yeah. Not so much when he opened the envelope, more when he read out the name.

WILLIAM. Yah, that's what I...

BECKHAM. Fact: in Russia one in every three professional football games is fixed. Fact: if you happen to be black, you can't set foot on a football pitch without someone chucking a banana at you. What with the African teams and all the South Americans, there's just going to be like... bananas everywhere. And Qatar! What's that about. Since when was that a country!

WILLIAM. Very homophobic apparently. It's illegal to be gay there.

BECKHAM. Yeah? So... bit of a worry then from a... from a Rex point of view...

WILLIAM. Sorry?

BECKHAM. It's okay. Apparently we'll be playing in temperatures of fifty degrees. It's tough enough being forty-three.

WILLIAM. Actually that's the 2022 bid...

BECKHAM. Oh right. Right! So I'll be...

*Beat.*

WILLIAM. Forty-seven.

*Pause.*

It's forty-seven, definitely forty...

BECKHAM. Forty-seven, yeah. Even worse. And you know the worsest thing of all... is I think this is all my fault.

WILLIAM. David…

BECKHAM. No really.

WILLIAM. David!

BECKHAM. I'm telling you.

WILLIAM. There's no such word as 'worsest'. But listen, don't beat yourself up.

Blimey, look at me. You're not the one who…

BECKHAM. I think I might have brung the wrong crystals.

WILLIAM. Brought.

BECKHAM. I mixed them up with the ones Victoria uses for her IBS.

WILLIAM. Right. Well, that might explain why David got rather hot under the collar.

*PENNY comes in carrying a pair of trousers.*

BECKHAM. That's the ones.

PENNY. Where is he?

*CAMERON comes out of the bedroom.*

CAMERON (*on phone*). No, well, you have to roll with the punches, don't you. Speak soon. Bye.

Success? Excellent. Thank you. (*Putting on the trousers.*) Well, the good news is, that whether or not he's a milkman, Lachlan O'Riley is definitely not working for News International and so far no one's heard of him anywhere else. Rebekah's going to call me back if she digs anything else up. So. All is not lost.

WILLIAM. Thank God for that.

CAMERON. Listen, chaps…

*He is dressed now in BECKHAM's slightly too tight trousers.*

...we have to head down to the press call in a couple of minutes. I know we've had our difficult moments, but I think we should let them all know out there that we really have all pulled together on this one. And whatever flak comes our way as it no doubt will, I really appreciate your hard work and dedication on this, and I'm just so sorry that when it came to it we were stitched up so comprehensively by... well, frankly by a bunch of second-rate crooks.

ASHOK *enters. He is carrying* WILLIAM*'s trousers.*

ASHOK. Your Royal Highness, Mr Beckham and Mr Cameron, I am so, so sorry. My brother Vikram... I told you before... he's not the full shilling. You see what he has done...

*He holds up the trousers to show a large hole in the seat.*

I told him to use a hairdryer and what does he do? He uses an iron.

WILLIAM. That was a rather expensive suit actually.

ASHOK. We've both let you down. First me, then my brother. I am so sorry, sir.

WILLIAM. Not to worry.

ASHOK. But I see you all have trousers!

CAMERON. Of a kind, yes. (*To the others.*) Listen, you guys go ahead. I'll see you down there.

PENNY. Shall I...?

CAMERON. No, no I'll catch you up.

WILLIAM (*to* BECKHAM *as they exit*). Oh by the way, yah, I had another chat with Kate about the wedding. The singing thing. Bit awkward but it turns out she's actually already had an offer from Paul McCartney? So...

BECKHAM. Fantastic! Even better.

WILLIAM. Oh. You think she'll be alright with that then?

BECKHAM. Yeah no problem. No problem at all.

WILLIAM. Thank God for that.

BECKHAM. So it'll be like a duet, yeah?

*WILLIAM, BECKHAM and PENNY exit.*

ASHOK. Any bags to go down, sir?

CAMERON. You know, Ashok, you're not going to like this, but when someone comes to write the very short chapter on England's failed bid and decides as they inevitably will that I'm the one to blame, what people won't take into account, I suspect, is the fact that I was sent in to bat with a pair of halfwits... Tweedle Dee and Tweedle Dum... and sadly two halfwits do not a whole wit make. In fact by some contradictory quirk of mathematics they make a quarter wit.

ASHOK. You really think so, sir?

*CAMERON's phone rings.*

CAMERON. I really think so. Excuse me a second.

*As CAMERON speaks, ASHOK checks the bedroom and the bathroom. He wheels out CAMERON's bag.*

*(On phone.)* Rebekah hello, sorry about all this... *(Beat.)* He really *is* a milkman, how extraordinary. Thank you so much, for reasons you will never know I cannot tell you how delighted I am to... *(Beat.)* What?

*(Beat.)* Who told you that? *(Beat.)* Who the bloody hell told you?

*(Beat.)* Because there were only the four of us here who knew...

*(Beat.)* Five, What do you mean five?

*CAMERON looks up to see ASHOK standing directly in front of him. He continues to listen to Rebekah for a moment and then lowers the phone, staring at ASHOK. ASHOK speaks... but this time in an English accent. He is very cheerful.*

ASHOK. Game up, is it? Never mind, job done.

CAMERON. Exactly how low can you lot sink?

ASHOK. A little bit lower than a banker but not quite as low as a politician.

CAMERON. I wish I'd stuck with Vikram now.

ASHOK. You shouldn't have sacked him then. Bloody hell, that nearly screwed things up. Still I didn't come all this way just to fall at the first fence. See, I thought Vikram would do the trick but I underestimated how much you lot like having your collective arse licked.

CAMERON. Yes alright, I get the picture. (*Points at the trousers*.) I assume you've told Rebekah about these.

ASHOK. Had to really. It would have been irresponsible not to. Small fry really in the great scheme of things but you never know. Surprisin' how much you pick up just standin' outside someone's door. Mind you I once nailed a foreign secretary for kiddie fiddlin' just by lip-readin'.

CAMERON. Lucky me.

ASHOK. I'll be off now unless there's anything else.

CAMERON. Yes of course, it must always be a bit awkward this bit.

ASHOK. Not really. Same as you. Just doin' my job. But you're right, they normally find out *after*. This is a bit unusual.

CAMERON. Yes. For me too. So what's it to be. What can I look forward to reading over tomorrow's breakfast?

ASHOK. What do you reckon? 'PM's intern bangs Aussie milkman in hotel bedroom.' Bit tame. I'm talkin' headlines obviously. How about 'Tweedle Dumb and Tweedle Dumber… what the PM *really* thinks.'

CAMERON. What does he want?

ASHOK. Who? Oh *him*.

CAMERON. Apart from my head on a platter.

ASHOK. Better ask him, I suppose. I'm just a foot soldier, me.

*He makes for the door.*

 I tell you one thing though.

CAMERON. What?

ASHOK. Whatever it is, you'll give it to him.

ASHOK *leaves the room.* CAMERON *stands for a moment. Then with an air of resignation he takes a deep breath and dials a number. Pause.*

CAMERON. Rupert, it's David... hello. (*Beat.*) Fine, absolutely fine. Have you got a minute? (*Beat.*) Yes, just wondered if we could bring Friday's meeting forward a little... (*Beat.*) How about this evening? (*Beat.*) Eight o'clock? (*Beat.*) Yes, it is quite urgent as it happens. (*Beat.*) Great, usual arrangements then, Number 10... (*Beat.*) Er no, back door (*Beat.*) *back* door... (*Beat.*) Rupert, we've been through this before, it has to be the back door... (*Beat.*) Because it does...

*Pause.*

Ah. So you've spoken to Rebekah already, have you? Right. Okay then, eight o'clock, this evening. (*Beat.*) Rupert! (*Beat. Resigned.*) Front door it is.

CAMERON *ends the call.*

One day...

*He suddenly kicks the football hard against the wall in frustration.*

*He grabs his bag and walks out of the room. Blackout.*

*The End.*

**www.nickhernbooks.co.uk**

facebook.com/nickhernbooks

twitter.com/nickhernbooks